He Loves Me, He Loves Me Knot
He Loves Me

A. R. Mullen

A. R. Mullen

1

He Loves Me, He Loves Me Knot, He Loves Me!

Acknowledgements

There is nothing greater than to be able to tell God THANK YOU for allowing me to publish my first book after holding onto it for many years. I wrote this book in 2006 yet I did not release it until now when God assured me that IT IS TIME. I thank him for my husband, *James J Mullen Jr.*, the man who held me tight in his strong and loving arms. Through many hours of hard work and tears he was faithful in encouraging me to reach my goals one day and one step at a time.

I also thank God for his anointed servant Pastor Joel Osteen who encouraged my heart from the beginning to the ending pages of this book. No, I do not know him, his beautiful wife Victoria or their children personally; however, their public lives are a reminder that with God all things are possible as they have generously shared with us through many awesome testimonies.

To my beloved mother
Rev. Joyce Harris who encouraged me to journal since I was a child. It helped me to express my thoughts and so much more.

To my eldest sister
Portia Gray-Goffigan, a very seasoned writer herself, who pushed and pushed so that I didn't sleep my blessing. Thank you Sistah!

To my beloved friends Anica & Reva my R.O.DS & BFFS! AKA ride or die girls & best friends. You inspired me in more ways than you could ever imagine. If I didn't know any better, I would think you were angels sent from heaven. Question, do angels turn up? (Smile)

To my childhood BFF Sandra Williams, a woman who watched me transition from the young journalist to the adult woman that I eventually became. She loves me unconditionally with my flaws and all, my Sandy Cakes! God knows what he is doing even in our youth.

This list can go on for hours. So I will end by saying I am thankful for the many people who kept me in their prayers: My late mother in law Esther Whitfield, my Dad, Deacon Walter Harris my eldest daughter Shamika, her husband Elvin Jr., my middle daughter Joy, my youngest daughter Nicole, to my sons James Sr., Antonio Jr., Garret, my future daughter in law Sharay, my beautiful grand-children, James Whitfield Jr., Jayda Lynn, Jarious and my unborn grandbaby. To my siblings, Emanuel, Patrick and my baby sister Stacey and to all of my nieces and nephews, my Auntie Donna, Auntie Melverine, Auntie Tiny, my god children Jer'Vonne, Jamaal, Danielle, DChina and so many more! Thank you for your Love for it has power to restore!

A. R. Mullen

Content

Introduction

He Loves Me, He Loves Me Knot, He Loves Me!

INTRODUCTION

Life Support Love....

He Loves Me, He Loves Me Knot, He loves me is an easy read. It doesn't take a rocket scientist to know what love is or to figure out that Jack and Maylene Frost had fallen out of love after thirty years. His actions revealed just how unhappy he was and his rare appearances were an indication that this home was no longer of interest. When he did drop in from time to time he was filled with negative comments and complaints. He bossed Mrs. Frost around as if she was his personal puppet. For a very long time she associated his displeasure with his hard career in law enforcement and the toll it took on him from day to day. She made excuses for his actions often when people would approach her with comments of infidelity and his long time away from home. Maylene was no fool. But their marital baggage was not up for discussion. Now if you were one of her closest friends she would have a hard time convincing you that they were still in love. In fact, it became a phrase of her's that marriage can be loveless. But, should they pull the plug? If so who would do it? Would it be the "lonely housewife" or the "I'm tired of my family husband?" It wasn't an easy decision; it is very similar to a loved one on life support. The family is challenged to make a decision to pull the plug. The doctor has reported that there is nothing left he or she can do and the insurance company will not approve another day of medical expenses because the hospital cannot justify the costs. All of the family members who are aware of this life threatening decision stand against the white sterile walls leaning for dear life. If someone was capable of moving the wall, all hell would break loose and their support would be loss. Not long following this catastrophe the answer would be revealed. It would come at a time when most people would say it was awkward. Read on and let us know your thoughts.

CHAPTER 1

The Christmas Catalog

Why am I flicking broke Again? Jack looked at his empty pockets that was turned inside out.

It was the day after Thanksgiving; Jack was on his way to the kitchen to get something to drink. While he was in route he tripped over a very thick Christmas catalog and he swore Maylene's name was written all over it. Was it left there on purpose or was this just a coincidence? In Jack's mind everything was purposed and you were guilty until you proved your innocence. From time to time he would let the words slip off of his tongue. "Why am I so flicking broke again?" Jack looked at his empty pockets that was turned inside out. Most times he blamed Maylene for influencing their children to rob him of everything that he earned. He said they didn't value him or his hard earned money and found numerous ways to spend it before he got paid. Christmas seemed to be stressful for him because he wanted to fulfill each of the children's wishes and still maintain the ongoing bills. So the catalogs were only a reminder that there was more money to be spent than Jack felt that the family had. He said this could have been avoided if Maylene just got rid of the books that had the

9

children in fantasy land. To Maylene it was every child's
dream to think of what they could have. This didn't mean they
were guaranteed to get each item on their wish list. But in the
same breath she would say it doesn't hurt to dream. In fact,
she told them it was important for them to know what they
wanted most and to check off the two items they especially
wanted and she and Jack would make the final decisions. Jack
didn't agree with this method. He said it made him look bad
and very cheap. He said the children's way around this rule
was to select more expensive items so that they would feel
their Christmas was worth wild. So how did this make
Maylene feel? She had mixed emotions. She wanted to see
the children smile but she wanted to see Jack less stressed. If
she could only convey to him her true wishes maybe they
wouldn't have so many fights and they could work harder on
their marriage. But Jack said he made a big mistake in getting
married and having so many children. This broke Maylene's
heart every time he said this and enough was enough.
What did he want from his wife? Simple understanding, he
would say. Maylene thought she was providing this but to him
she was the true culprit. Everything he spoke of that related to
their marriage was negative and he soon made his feelings
public. Whenever they would have company he would share
unpleasant comments that would make the people around them
very uncomfortable. Maylene wracked her brain trying to find
ways to keep him happy. She thought maybe if I do this or that
he won't feel a need to humiliate me. Yes, to the world at large
she was spoiled and had everything she wanted. But what she
wanted most of all was her husband's love and respect. She
received neither. She could not figure out how to make this
happen without losing herself in the interim. Eventually it was

suggested that she make her final decision by writing out the pros and cons of the marriage and she did this on one cold winter morning. When she completed the task it was unfortunate that the evil outweighed the good. At this point she knew the decision was made. She seen some real truths on the paper that she ignored for quite some time. The only way they would survive was if they took the initiative to make some important changes. When she approached Jack when he arrived home late from work one night he said it wasn't the right time to address her concerns. He said he didn't plan on changing and he was who he was, take him or leave him. This infuriated Maylene. She had taken so much time to try to give the marriage one more chance. Maybe she wasn't direct enough. Maybe he didn't understand what Maylene was truly trying to convey. Standing tall and confident on the outside, yet shaking on the inside she got up enough nerve to attempt to discuss the subject one more time.

Maylene: Ok Jack, I won't take too much of your time. The point that I am trying to make is where do we go from here? Get a divorce or try to make this marriage work? So that I am clear in what you are saying I believe you are telling me you do not plan on changing your behavior that conflicts with the vows you made to me thirty years ago.

Jack: You are correct my dear. This is exactly what I am saying. All you do is sit at home doing nothing and expect me to do everything. At the bare minimum I need to have some down time for myself. If this means hurting you, then so be it.

I have been pleasing everyone but myself. Again I am who I am, take me or leave me."

Maylene: "I guess you forgot who has held this family down when you had nothing. It's funny how I was the perfect wife when I jumped at your command and supported this family when you lost your job and couldn't buy this family a loaf of bread. But I humbled myself for five years and even helped you pay your child support for a child that was conceived out of infidelity. If I am not a good woman to you get your stuff and leave so God can send me someone who knows a good woman when he sees one.

With widened eyes Maylene could not believe the words that came out of her mouth. Looking side eyed she said "did I say that?"

Jack: I am not going anywhere. Who do you think is paying the bills?"

Maylene: If you think that's what makes you a good man ask yourself what is a man's reasonable service. You're not doing us a favor, you are being the head of the household as you so eloquently broadcast every time you get a chance.

Jack: Ohhhh, a bible quote huh? Did I miss something? When did you become this holy woman?

Maylene: Not holy, but knowledgeable. You cannot make me feel guilty for expecting you to do your part for our family.

You go out and work and you asked me to quit my government job to stay at home and work. I.e. to run this daily empire we call home and family.

Jack: It's funny how you can include the bible when you want. You are so selective! But we both know you are NOT PERFECT!

Maylene: YES, YOU'RE COR-RECT! I am super far from perfect. So much so that I am constantly asking you what I have done that keeps you so angry. You won't tell me what the problem is. How can I correct what I do not know?

Jack: You would have to be an idiot to not recognize what your problem is.

Maylene: Oh, my problem huh and an idiot….is this what you think of me? The name calling hurts me Jack. I'm trying to talk to you in a cordial manner. Do you want to discuss this or what? Jack looked at Maylene with mere discuss as if he hated to even hear her voice. There was a strong lull; neither Jack nor Maylene had anything to say. All of a sudden Maylene had an epiphany as the tears rolled down her face. "Maylene" she said to herself, "you cannot change what is out of your control. Remember you said this before and he has done nothing to change. So, in other words it's time to move on. Then she walked away. Maylene had developed a limp and had difficulties standing for long periods of time. She wondered if it came from the many hours she had to stand on her feet doing odd jobs to keep a little change in her pocket. As time progressed the pain grew. Eventually Maylene sought medical attention and was told there was a great chance she was suffering the after mass of her former car accident as a child. She thought this would affect her ability to make it on her own if she and Jack went their separate ways.

This was a very scary thought however she had to get prepared to go it alone. Thankfully Maylene developed many talents over the years. She home schooled children in their neighborhood, created a home salon, developed an interior design empire and took many college classes that was offered at a discounted rate. Eventually she became well known in her community for these talents and she soon contracted with various businesses and families. But this didn't last long before Jack complained that the jobs took too much of Maylene's time. She found it impossible to please him when she attempted to help with the smaller expenses that they incurred such as the costs of the children's sport camps, uniforms and the numerous field trips to say the least. He gave her no credit for her contribution and he joked that he could make her measly money in one day that she took weeks to earn. Did he say this because it bothered him that she was helping at all or did he want her to rely on him? Did she become too independent? It was hard for her to tell. But his answer would follow with drastic actions and the list was pretty extensive. She heard of other housewives experiencing like situations but she never thought it would be her. How could someone who said they loved you treat you worse than he did the family dog? Oh boy, I better get ready for the storm she thought. I'm so glad I took those classes online while he was at work to further my skills. Who knew that it was the right time to explore options of independence? My gosh, is this really happening? I didn't want it to really come to this. She was now panicking about what was a mere thought in the past. She constantly studied about the new products on the market that helped painters prefect their work. She learned interior designer tips so that she could make her designs have great appeal. She practiced hair art on her best clients known as their children. They were her advertisement as they were also her biggest supporters. "Mama you can do anything huh" their little girl Autumn use to say. In Maylene's mind she would think "Not everything little girl,….seems I can't keep your father at home." But she didn't let this slip out. They were Autumn's biggest heroes. Now looking at her projection table that she had planted in her mental catalog of numbers, "I bet I can save up enough money to survive if I only plan wisely. But this time did not come. Instead weeks went by before Maylene could regroup from the many interruptions that fleeted her door**. Have you ever made plans that were interrupted?**

He Loves Me, He Loves Me Knot, He Loves Me!

CHAPTER 2
INTERRUPTED

…. Three weeks later

Clyde was out of breath and speaking very fast. All of his words seemed to be running together and a bit hard for Maylene to follow.

The weather forecast had come true. On every neighboring television it read in big letters "WINTER STORM WARNING-SCHOOL AND BUSINESS CLOSINGS LISTED BELOW." This is a stay at home mother's nightmare come true. Not another snow day…. they groaned. This was a universal sign for why me? But that was the least of Mrs. Frost's worries. Why were there three robust officers standing outside of her window next to their shiny black vehicle conversing about who knows what? The Frost family would soon find out. Yup, sooner than not. The Frost kids sat on the first floor of their Victorian home. They were watching the news report for the surrounding cities and towns and were surprised at how many school closings appeared on the flat screen. The older adult children explained how it was when they were younger. How school would not be closed unless there was a literal blizzard,

17

not a blizzard warning. The superintendent would make house calls to announce that all schools would be open until further notice. They laughed and laughed until they couldn't laugh any more. After taking a brief break they would resume laughing and storytelling once again.

Winter and Summer looked at Autumn and said do you like to make snow angels? Just as she was about to answer the flashing lights from the police cars caught their brother Clyde's attention. Prior to this he was opening his mail and complaining about the horrid experience that he was having as an adult and having to be responsible for his bills. "Where has the time gone he said as he walked over to the family room window?" He was taken back by what he witnessed and then he went running. This was a day that they dreaded but their father seemed to try to prepare them with many warnings. He would often say "May, I know you do not want to hear this but it comes with the territory." Without telling his siblings what he saw he ran swiftly up the spiral stairway screaming "MAMA come quickly!!!!" Maylene peaked out of her tall French doors to see why her son was screaming.

Maylene: "Clyde what's going on?"

Clyde was out of breath and speaking very fast. All of his words seemed to be running together and a bit hard for Maylene to follow.

Clyde: "Mama they are here! They were the same officers who reported to Aunt Susie that Uncle was gone. All of their badges are covered in black tape. Clyde looked as if he'd seen a ghost. Maylene did not want to believe what he was attempting to say. Without him being as candid as he could have been she understood clearly what he meant. Maylene grabbed her plush white robe and tied it for dear life. Then she walked slowly to the staircase and seen all of her children at the bottom of the stairwell with saddened eyes. No, Clyde did not get to tell the entire details that he shared with their mother. But it didn't take a scientist to figure out what was going on. Maylene proceeded down the spiral stairs with fear in her eyes. Her children didn't know what to do except be by her side. It was as if they were frozen while the officers stood outside their home. So Maylene would eventually answer the infamous knock that continued on the other side of the door. Jack Jr. was visiting and in the laundry room folding his clothes. When he heard all of the commotion he rushed to see what was going on. He automatically went into protective mode as he was always taught to protect his mother and family in the absence of their dad. So he walked bravely to the door and Maylene stood behind her six-foot-tall son. When the door was opened wide enough for the family to see what stood on the other side they were relieved to see that it was their Uncle Bentley who was not their biological uncle but a very dear friend of the family. He served many years in law enforcement with their dad. With a very serious voice he said,

19

Officer Bentley: "Morning Frost family we are here on official business and I need to speak with Mrs. Frost alone." It was strange to hear Uncle Ben speak in this tone. The family never had odds against one another and for the most part they shared happy memories. But on this day they were far from cheery. Uncle Bentley had work to do and would not stop until it was done.

Maylene eased her way from behind their son and was relieved to see several familiar officers outside the door.

Then she chuckled as she shivered a bit from the cold air and offered the men to come inside.

Maylene: Oh my goodness guys come in. The kids and I thought you were the police bringing us bad news. Lol! Although Maylene wished that it was a light hearted matter the very still and quiet room was a reminder it was not a laughing matter at all. So it seemed the family's thoughts were correct? Bentley could feel a lump in his throat and had severe cotton mouth when he tried to speak. Who would have thought this tall stocky man who was built like a bull would have difficulty talking to a family that he knew so well? This was his sensitive side. Who knew there was such a thing? With tears in his eyes he outstretched his right hand to Mama and she witnessed the black tape across his badge. Then one of the officers whispered:

Officer: Glad the chief sent the group of us. He knew this might not go too well considering he's one of our own.

Maylene heard this when she barely touched Bentley's hand then she fell hard to the floor. BOOM!!!! It all happened so fast. What now? All of the kids ran over to their mother. School being out was now the last thing on any of their minds. "Why us they cried out?" There was wailing in the hollow entryway. It sounded like a very large echo. Their oldest daughter got her composure and ran to dial 911. She explained to the operator the nature of her call. It didn't take long before the paramedics and fire department was at their door. It was the scariest day of their lives. Were they losing two parents in one day? Who would have thought? Although Maylene had in her mind that she and Jack would not be together forever she didn't intend on losing him to death. In the meantime, the paramedics had a job to do and then off they went to the local hospital. The man who sat in the rear of the ambulance continued to take Maylene's vital signs. He did this as Winter prayed for her mother in a foreign tongue that made him fear that she might throw some magic dust on him or something.

Paramedic: Mam are you ok? He asked as he leaned to the side as if he was dodging a bullet.

Winter put one finger up gesturing that he waited a minute. Then she looked at him as if he asked her the most ridiculous question.

Paramedic: Bill, I may need your help back here, he said with concern.

21

Paramedic 2: Looking into his rearview mirror. Ok buddy, we are almost at the hospital.

Paramedic 1 tried hard to not show Winter he was concerned about her mom. However, the unknown babble made him fear more for his life than for her mother's. But nevertheless he had a work to do and he knew he had to remain professional. When they reached the hospital he couldn't help but rush to get Maylene out of the ambulance and into the ER where there was a room reserved for her. You would have thought that he was running from a monster as he pushed the hospital gurney down the hall. Did Winter know that she made this guy nervous? The nurses laughed over in their station.

Nurse 1: He's new and inexperienced. He hasn't seen nothing yet.

Nurse 2: I know huh? They laughed and laughed until Winter gave them a look of death. She didn't think her mother's medical state was a laughing matter. If they knew what Winter was thinking they would have left well enough alone. It wasn't safe for them to even giggle; Winter was waiting for the opportunity to call Jesus on them all. She mumbled under her breath, in the name of JESUSSSSS.....The emphasis on the "s" sounded like a hissing snake that forced the nurses who were congregating to practically trample each other like a herd of cows.

Then there was the doctor. He was waiting to see Maylene. She was top priority. The medical staff worked together to undress Maylene to give the doctor full access to her as it related to her condition. Winter was very guarded and made it clear that they not ask her to leave the hospital room. After Maylene was fully examined, her doctor explained to winter that her mother was in shock. The devastating news was too much for her to bear and the doctor wanted her to be admitted for observation. Winter was told that she was welcomed to stay with her mother.

It wasn't long before her ride -or- die Arie arrived on the scene. She looked as if she wanted to kill. What happened to her friend? The answers weren't coming fast enough. Somebody better talk real fast. Winter felt it should be her. She didn't want her Auntie to get caught in the handcuffs of the hospital police. They couldn't bare another tragic episode that day.

Winter: Auntie, Auntie, its ok, its okkk, the doctor said she is in shock she is alive. It is not as bad as it looks but we have to wait to see how Mama will be when she awakes. It all happened in seconds Auntie. I am so afraid……

Aries: I know niece, I know, come here. She held Winter so tight. Arie didn't know her strength. She treated her nieces and nephews like her own. She wouldn't let anything happen to them within her power.

23

Arie: Winter your siblings told me what happened. I am so sorry about your Dad. We are going to make it through this I promise niece. I promise you, okay?

Arie wanted to console all of the kids but was confused herself. Why didn't Maylene tell her that Jack wasn't doing well? Arie wandered how could she not see his health was deteriorating? The last thing she heard was Maylene and Jack was stressed about bills and Christmas. But obviously this was not the extent of it. She had no idea that things were so bad. She did not dare ask Winter or her sibling's further questions. She thought it would be better if she asked Winter at a later time. But how would she start her investigation? She wasn't trying to make matters worse. But she did want some answers. What was happening to this couple who loved each other so much? Just as she was about to ask Winter what really happened the doctor told them to be sure to converse outside of the room to prevent Maylene from getting upset. He said there was a chance she could hear everything they said. So Winter called her into the hallway to update her on what she missed. "The doctor said Mama will need to stay in the hospital so that she could be under a doctor's care. Apparently my brothers told you what they could and we are all still in shock ourselves. We did not see this coming. Our parents are way too young for this."

"I agree niece. None of us did. Although we know stress and holidays are the number one killers for most families. But do not worry God is going to handle all of this. Just watch and

see. Then she pulled Winter closer to her and again she attempted to reassure her that everything would be alright. However, the truth be told, Arie was as unsure about this situation as the next person. As always you never expect it to be you. **The "NEVER ME MOVEMENT" can you identify?**

He Loves Me, He Loves Me Knot, He Loves Me!

CHAPTER 3

DISCHARGED

Tears rolled down her cheeks and she did not say a word. She didn't need to they all knew what she was thinking and they did their best to prevent any direct memories from resurfacing.

Mama was away for a few days before she was discharged from the hospital. By grace the doctor gave her permission to leave after she was finally in the safe zone. But if it was up to her sister Paris she would have stayed in the hospital a couple of days longer. She didn't want to see her sister relapse from doing better to doing worse. But Winter assured her that their mother was ready to get in her own bed and she promised to let the family help her deal with their loss. While Winter was at the hospital gathering her Mother's belongings, her husband Rafee called to see if they were ready to be picked up. At this same time the church support was at the house asking how they could be of service. Summer appreciated their efforts but she and her siblings got

27

everything together that they could without the oldest
daughter Winter at the house guiding them as she did when
they were children.

Sister Washboard: Summer don't worry about it being a
problem this is what the church is supposed to do. When there
is a grieving family in need it is our duty to be there to help
even if you are not faithful to God and never pay your tithes.
But this is beside the point. Please forgive me. Will you tell us
what we can do? We want to make things easier for all of you.

Summer: No Mam we did everything yesterday. We're all set,
thank you so much! We do appreciate how the church sent
over some food. We can smell it upstairs. That must be
Mother Franklin's chicken and dumplings. I know that aroma
from anywhere.

Sister Washboard: Yes, my dear you are correct. It is her
recipe. I know that your mother and father both loved her
home cooked meals even when they didn't come to her funeral.
But this is beside the point. We know this should put a smile
on your mother's face." This woman was getting on
Summer's dern nerves but she didn't want to appear
ungrateful.

Summer: Ms. I do not want to seem like we do not appreciate
your help, but I just remembered something. Could you please
get rid that food? Dad loved to eat this with Mom. This will
only make her even more emotional than she already is. They

ran to open the windows to get the aroma out of the house. But it was too late. Mama was soon home and brought directly up to her room. Tears rolled down her cheeks and she did not say a word. She didn't need to they all knew what she was thinking and they did their best to prevent any direct memories from resurfacing. But unfortunately this was near impossible. Everything she looked at in the house reminded her of her husband of thirty years. Who could help her from being emotional? No one knew how long this pain would last. They just had to accept this was a part of the grieving process.
How do you deal with loss?

He Loves Me, He Loves Me Knot, He Loves Me!

CHAPTER 4

WHAT YOU GET

Arie looked from side to side and put her strong hands around Tangerine's throat. She shook her and shook her until Tangerine stopped breathing but Arie still didn't let her go. It took four officers to remove her hands and CPR to resuscitate Tangerine. They could have arrested Arie but for some reason it seemed they thought Ms. Tangerine got what she deserved. Have you ever experienced this? Have you ever thought?

The church was so gracious in their giving during the Frost's loss. They had much experience with grieving families and did everything they possibly could to help the family through this time. The Frost family hadn't been as active in the church in the latter part of Mr. & Mrs. Frost's marriage. They argued most times and the children felt like they were in the middle of Chaos Central, the kids preferred to be less knowledgeable about their parent's silent or not so silent battles. But nevertheless they were and what do you do with this information? Your parents, the people who you put your most trust in, seem to be out of control. What now? Who plays the role of the responsible person? I guess this is to be determined. It is not long into the morning that Miss Buttons, the funeral director's daughter, walks out of Maylene's home office and asks the family to review the program that the church administrators put together. It was very brief and the family was pleased with the outcome. There was no need to drag out the details. The family thanked Miss Buttons and the team continuously for their ongoing support. This time was much harder than they would have imagined but some equipped people came along to do what they do best. There was a count down before the actual service would take place. This moment of life was dreaded by many but the true facts still remained. Jack was gone……

Many people came out to the service. Some said they found it unusual when they heard that there was such a compassionate church involved. They had seen many grieving families even more distressed because of the financial battles that came with the territory. They heard and experienced horror stories where money was the dominating factor than their loss. But this church knew how to address this matter because finances are definitely a part of the process involving such services. It is not what you say but how you say it that can really make a difference. The Frost family appreciated their training. It was evident they came from good teaching. As a result, the service was outstanding because people felt the liberty to express just how they felt. Not about the financial ticket that came with this battle. Hey, we have enough to worry about. Deal with this worry later. It was like a family reunion. People came from near and far. Little Autumn took out her small note pad and recorded all the states that she seen on each vehicle. Massachusetts, Virginia, Florida, Maryland, New York and many, many more. She was fascinated with all the people who said they were there for her family.

They hugged and reminisced right in the parking lot.

"How's your mother? I was sad when I heard that she'd fallen."

"She's doing much better we are taking it one day at a time."

"Hey Dude!" the very big guys said to one another in unison. "You better not grow any more or you will be declared a giant!"

There were so many conversations like these. Autumn couldn't grasp how many people loved her family.

Wow she thought my dad touched many lives. Boy he really made a difference......

Then she overheard a group of females talking about forgiving one another for being at odds because they all had a personal interest in her dad.

33

A mistress: Man, this is not what I wanted for this family. I see now the pain that they are in after losing their father and his wife losing her husband. Tears ran down the lady's face. Just to think we all have been home wreckers and during the short lived affairs we thought about no one but ourselves. But, looking at how devastated death can be on many people we have a responsibility stop doing wrong. Then they were interrupted by one of the ushers.

Usher: Hello everyone, the services will begin shortly.

"Ok, ok" many responded. Then they all begin to move toward the church entrance. There were numerous officers dressed in their blues. They were intimidating yet it showed they respected the family.

People paused to look at the many picture collages in the church vestibule. Some were included in the memories while others wondered why they were not.

Then the services begin. It was extremely emotional. It was hard keeping people on task because their emotions took over. They shared how much the family affected their lives. It seemed more was said about Jack and Maylene together than about the one who they were about to bury.

A mistress: To each of you, who have disrespected this couple in any way, take the time to remember this could be you on this front bench because God doesn't like ugly. I know from personal experience you can't do wrong and expect things to

34

go right. My children heard about this loss and they are so angry with me. She broke down in tears. She seemed so hurt. Not because of the loss of Jack but also because of the death it brought on the family.

Mistress: People…I have lost my family. They have called me a pure harlot. They found out he was a married man and I am the fault of this. I chose to have an affair with a married man. I did it. Now I regret what I did. People are stoning me and my children. My children are innocent. Look what I have done. They look at me as if I am nothing. Mrs. Frost I am soooo, soooo sorry.

Summer: Oh my gosh! What in the world are we dealing with? Is this some sort of joke? Who would take this time to bring further humiliation to this family? At this time, you could hear a pin drop and not for good reasons. Then the minister walked up to the podium and gestured to the sound guy to turn off the lady's microphone.

Then Mother Frost, Jack's mother got up and gave her testimony. She talked about being in this young lady's position and the pain it brought her family. The curse that hung over them because of her past decisions. She beckoned other people in the room to promise themselves they would make every effort to not curse their families. She began to cry.

Mother Frost: I saw this coming. I tried to warn my son and my daughter to find peace with God so that he could order their steps. But their ongoing home life grew more and more stressful and believe me, I know from seventy-five years of life that stress can make you or break you. A wise man once said in Roman 12, I can't member the verse just yet, but do not be conformed to the pattern of this world, but be ye transformed by the renewing of your mind. Then you will be able to test and approve what God's will is—his good, pleasing and perfect will.

A Professional Mourner who could cry on the drop of a dime: Powerful, just powerful, she said as she nodded her head in agreeance. We need a new way of thinking. I totally agree.

Then the usher's a.k.a. her grandchildren came and escorted her back to her seat. The room was in tears by this time. Wisdom showed up as she was needed. Moments went by and it was now time for the service to come to a close. The Pastor gave final words and the funeral director lead the people.

As the guests were leaving many gave sincere condolences and expressed their total surprise to the family's loss. Several of Jack's coworkers said they were shocked since he never gave them a clue of what he was going through.

Mr. Backandforth, Jack's coworker extended his hand to the broken   Mrs. Frost and offered to be available should she need him.

Mrs. Backandforth grabbed his arm as if she was taking his blood pressure. Ouchhh he whispered. "Why did you squeeze me so tight? Did you lose your balance or something?" Mrs. Backandforth just gave him a you know why look and he must have understood because he did not ask any further questions.

Mr. Backandforth: May, before we leave we wanted to give you this bouquet of Roses. I know Jack use to send you flowers every Friday. We brought you these with hopes that it would bring you as much cheer as can be expected. He extended his hand and passed them to Maylene. Arie stood next to her as if she was the Gestapo ready to give just about anyone who got in her way an immediate beat down. She checked the flowers for bugs because she didn't trust anyone. But she soon learned Mr. Backandforth was just trying to honor Maylene as a grieving widow who lost her husband. What he didn't know was the flowers Jack sent out every Friday were not for his wife. Maylene thought in her mind, Thanks Jack, you have given me the strength to go on knowing I shouldn't miss such a cheater. There were many who revealed truths that were unknown to Maylene all in the name of innocence. They shared office stories and the many encounters Jack had with his various family members. But most of Jack's biological family was from the south and they were nowhere to be found. So the people who called themselves relatives were in fact Jack's crew of females who served as his free barber, therapist and faithful masseuse. But Maylene kept her thoughts to herself and thanked them for their ongoing efforts in helping her family and prayed God would bless each of them. However,

Ms. Tangerine, Jack's biggest cheerleader seemed to come from out of nowhere as she swung her big hips around the room. Despite the earlier warning she still felt a need to blurt out her thoughts.

Ms. Tangerine: HEY, I GOTTA A QUESTION PEOPLE, what happens to a person who has wounds beyond repair? Her tone denoted more sarcasm than one should handle at such a time as this. Arie, Maylene's ride or die got in her face and looked down on Tangerine.

Arie: Talking through her teeth she asked, gotta question huh Ms. Nasty?

Tangerine: Kinda sorta if I may add. From my point of view this woman was beneath him and if it was up to me he would have exited long before this!

Arie looked from side to side and put her strong hands around Tangerine's throat. She shook her and shook her until Tangerine stopped breathing but Arie still didn't let her go. It took four officers to remove her hands and CPR to resuscitate Tangerine. They could have arrested Arie but for some reason it seemed they thought Ms. Tangerine got what she deserved. Have you ever experienced this? ***Have you ever thought to yourself, that's exactly what they get?***

Hours later at the Repass.....

Now the family was home and the house is filled with so many people. Some who the children knew while others they were not familiar. The Frost family never imagined they would be able to fill their very large home as they did on that day. Maylene received hugs and kisses like she never had before. But it wasn't until she received the best hug of all. It was her OLD LOVE who came to give his condolences. Her eyes filled with tears and he lifted her into his arms. He held her as if he was her long lost father. But this wasn't the case at all. Maylene had a wonderful dad who was in her corner during this pivotal time. But this was the man who proposed to her while she was pregnant with another man's child. This was decades ago. But the family loss brought them back together again. Old times began to cross her mind. She wandered how could she tell this man who had been in her corner that she betrayed his trust? Could she tell him thank you for being there from the same tongue that was used to lie to him? Would he believe her? Did she hurt him enough that he should have forgotten her name and never looked back? He was the epitome of a respectable man. Why do some females wish to accept a man who shows them no respect? Why do we openly invite heartache and forfeit our blessings? Kinda crazy huh? Well this was Maylene's story. She met a young man in her youth one day in choir rehearsal. Some called him a nerd because he seemed like a square among circles. Eventually they became close friends and found laughter in just about anything. So much so, the choir director separated them because she said they were having too much fun. But right after rehearsal they would hang out together. People said they were inseparable. But the mothers of the church said to them it looked like puppy love. That was until Jack came on the scene and squoze his way in between them.

Jack: Excuse me, cuse me, cuse me, said his body language as G became a focus of the past. Maylene was now more interested in another tall nerd who dressed differently from her other peers. He stood out from the crowd. He was smart and had big whit and could make you laugh until it hurt. He had charisma. But no one knew this but his close family and friends. This saddened G that he was put on the back burner. He was like a third wheel that was in the far distance of the crowd. But he never disappeared from the picture even though Maylene acted as if he wasn't there.

Jack: Hey who is that dude always standing in the background?

Maylene: Oh he is JUST a friend.

How soon she forgot the joy that Gentleman brought her early on. It's funny how we can put someone on the back burner when we think we found someone better. But it wasn't long before Maylene was in G's position when Jack found his new pretty young thing. This was after they decided they would be a young couple. Then one of his boys introduced him to his girl and she left him for Jack. Go figure! So Jack and Maylene went their separate ways until Jack seen Maylene at a local block party. He wasn't happy about the guys who were circling his old girl. But he had a nerve he was already taken. The music was blaring and this meant nothing to the young people. The vibration of the music made you feel like you were in the eye of a storm. But drugs and alcohol made all of this invisible. Jack walked over to Maylene and offered her a toke of his illegal cigarette. Instead of declining she accepted his offer and was soon in his sports car driving down the road to nowhere. When they arrived at nowhere he offered her a drink. Neither of them were of legal age to consume alcohol yet they dranked as if they were pros. Soon they were engaged in unprotected sex. That's right, sex. Something neither of them knew very much about although they thought they were so smart. What came next would show everyone just how experienced they were. Not only to themselves but to the world at large. People would know now that they made a mistake. Why did she allow this to happen? This was one incident that she could not apologize away. It would change her life drastically. That choir girl would be looked at differently. The spot light that would shine on her now was not pleasing to her parents, her siblings, clergy, her teachers and all of the people that held her to a high standard. WHAT A DRASTIC MISTAKE! She would be dressed in the same clothes of shame as some of her peers. The shame of being an

41

unwed mother at a very young age. My gosh, she and her English teacher were due to have their babies in the same month. But this wasn't Maylene's biggest concern. She also had to tell the young man who loved her that she was pregnant with another man's baby. She would have to tell him she cheated on him when he trusted her most. WOW! If she could turn the clock back her beautiful baby girl could have shared the love of a wonderful man who was willing to stand in the gap. Instead he was devastated when he seen her growing belly. She treaded lightly when she spoke with him during this time. She didn't know how she would tell him. But finally she did and he reacted differently from what she expected. Instead he got down on one knee and told her that he forgave her and he asked her to be his bride.

Maylene: What about the baby?

G: I will raise the child as my own.

Then he waited for Maylene to respond. He was more mature than the average male his age. He had experience in being treated differently and knew the heartache this could bring. He was empathetic and wanted to be there for his dear friend.

Some said he was empathetic because he made mistakes of his own. That he also brought shame on his parents and wished he could take back his actions as well. But this wasn't true. It was pure gossip to add to the buzz of that time. His concern was for Maylene and being there for her when she needed him most.

Question: Are we supposed to be there for the people we love? Does this only apply to romantic relationships? If a person is not as devoted would you say they never loved you at all? Was this an extreme case? Some have said yes. It's funny, some said Maylene felt Manny (aka G) was there for her more than her own parents?

Maylene was having flash backs of her dad screaming at her older sister at the top of his lungs. Or at least this is how it sounded to her as she eased dropped from the wall adjacent to the front parlor of their home.

Maylene's Dad: PARISSSSS, LISTEN AND LISTEN CLEARLY! WE ARE NOT GOING TO RAISE ANY MORE CHILDREN AND THIS MEANS NO -GRAND- CHILD-RENNNNN YOU GET ME? Maylene's mother: Nodding as she stood behind their dad with her arms crossed.

Paris: DAD, I do not have a clue of what you are talking about. Why are you saying this to me?

Maylene's Dad: WELL LET'S BEGIN WITH THE STORY MS. EDDIE TOLD ME AND YOUR MOTHER. WHAT WERE YOU DOING WITH THAT BOY AT THE COMMUNITY CENTER?
Paris: Looking dumbfounded…Oh my gosh! Is that your source? Whatever she said is not true because I do not go to the Community Center.

Maylene's Dad: WHY WOULD THIS OLD WOMAN LIE ON YOU? TELL ME WHY?

Paris: I guess she told you this because you and Ma are an easy target and she loves to start drama.

Maylene's Dad: ARE YOU CALLING US GULLIBLE? HUH? WE WERE BORN AT NIGHT BUT NOT LAST NIGHT. GRRRRRR... From where Maylene stood it looked like her parents were about to ring her sister's neck and they were going in for the kill. What she got from this was "You better not get pregnant or ELSE! It behooved her to take G at his offer. She felt worthless and she was thankful that Manny wouldn't let her go this journey alone. But she didn't feel like this for long. She broke off their engagement when Jack came to his senses and took the responsibility of getting this young girl pregnant and he eventually married her and she expected to live a happily ever after. But the love affair ended as all good things come to an end. Now G's back after twenty plus years. Is this love or was he a glutton for punishment? Unlike the people who will kick you when you are down, he opted to be the one to extend his hand to give her a help up. The people in the room looked at the great rapport she had with this man on sight. They began to whisper that he must be the lover some said she had before she lost Jack. Some didn't care if she heard them or not.

2ⁿᵈ Professional Mourner: Hey Alabama, talking about cheaters, I guess he is the one her mother in law was referring

44

to in her remarks. She said they both were in trouble. She said this as she raised her left brow.

Alabama: Mmmm, I didn't hear her say that.

2nd Professional Mourner: Well I am going with mother. Heck she has lived with them for a while and I bet she knows what she is saying.

People began to gather their things. They were not comfortable with what they seen. But Mother Buttonup said be careful how you judge. You don't know her story. As she handed the guests their coats she said thank you for coming to be in support of our grieving family. Everyone grieves differently. Grief comes in different shapes and sizes.

Is there a "wrong way" to grieve?

He Loves Me, He Loves Me Knot, He Loves Me!

CHAPTER 5
BACK AT YA!
3 week later……

Sonwa: I'm going up to that hospital to wrap those IV cords around her neck!"

Maylene: Oh nooooo, you have way too much going for you to let your life be destroyed further by this sicko! Trust me I know your pain. But believe me she wasn't just sleeping with your husband. Sonwa stopped suddenly in her tracks. She looked at Maylene. Then she paused for what felt like a while.

Maylene: "SUMMER AND AUTUMN COME ON, TIME TO GO!"

Autumn ran to Summer's room and shook her until she was awake.

Autumn: Sister where are we going? Mama said get ready to go. Go where?

47

Summer: Looking up from her designer pillows all lined up in a row. What are you talking about? Then she covered her head with her favorite one.

Just as she completed her sentence there stood their mother standing in the doorway.

Maylene: What are you girls doing? You should be dressed by now. Hurry up; you will make me late for my job!

Summer: With a frown …Huh Mummma? What job? She said this as she slid out of the bed with her long pink socks against her light gray sweat pants. She knew she better not attempt to have this conversation without showing she was moving with a purpose. Yet she didn't know what in fact this purpose was.

Maylene: These bills are not going to disappear on their own. I received three requests to paint and redesign three sanctuaries and two parsonages. You know I will need your help. I told you this on yesterday!

Summer moved fast to gather some clothes and off to the Jack and Jill bathroom she went. She didn't talk back to her mother but she did not recall them having this conversation. She wasn't alone, neither did Autumn. They were soon ready to go and this assignment felt like old times.
But for Maylene it wasn't a good road down memory lane. To her, she was reminded of the many awful arguments she and Jack had because he did not value her worth. He would brag about all that he did for the family and how her hard work in

the home was as invaluable as the stranger on the street. So she built her silent empire of businesses to maintain the lifestyle that they built for the family together yet at times he would take the good life away from them when he felt like it.
For example, he would tell her last minute the children would not be able to play on one of the sports teams after they were told they could and they worked extra hard around the house to show their dad that they appreciated him affording the expenses. But Maylene would be left to give the bad news. She would have to cancel the wonderful days they anticipated enjoying with their peers and their friend's families. The road trips and meet and greets would be out of the question. The expenses for the uniforms alone would be unaffordable. Maylene was sad and embarrassed that Jack had this kind of power over her. She would stay away from him to keep from having explosive arguments. She didn't like to see a grown man being a coward and using her to bare bad news. This is how she felt even if it wasn't true. Was he really facing a hardship as he mentioned and couldn't afford the added expenses? After seeing the receipts of his extracurricular activities she realized she was actually correct. He wasn't manning up and left her to wipe away their tears. He had some kind of nerve when he thought he could climb in the bed and attempt to be romantic. She saw him as an infected being that cared about no one but himself. She could still smell the scent of sex on his body. He was depleted. This always confirmed her suspicions.
As much as she wanted to turn her head all she could think about was a female being raped. She felt helpless and she imagined trying to get herself out of the strong arms of this

49

strange man's body. She was a victim and he was the assailant. What would be the long term results of his actions? In some cases, there were females who claimed they were carrying his child although he denied the allegations. But to Maylene it meant unprotected relations and behaviors unchanged. She was no dummy despite what he thought of her. On that morning all she could recall was the times she would stand in tears writing down her get away strategies. She hated the horrible memories. The dreadful feeling of being single after being married for thirty years was a dreadful truth. She would chant in her mind just leave Jack, just leave him, but she didn't know the pain that would follow. Many things crossed her mind while she waited for her girls. Did she bring this pain on herself or was it God's timing to bring her change no matter how bad it hurt? For a moment she thought what she would do to have his cheating self with her for one more day. She thought about why so many of her elders stayed the marital course with their wandering eye husbands. She knew she had to find a way to use this as a strength so she pulled herself together and thanked him for his faults because she was forced to make it on her own. She was now gung-ho to get the assignment done. She and the girls got to the sight and in no time the work was done. Maylene and her clients were very pleased with the outcome. As they were leaving the job she received an unexpected call. It was her former friend who she hadn't seen or spoken with in quite a while. This was on purpose because of how her former friend began to treat her around the inner circle. Maylene decided she deserved better friends and would allow herself to become acquainted with the network clubs in her area. Then without thinking Maylene answered the call. She was not happy about those ripe old reflexes. She really didn't want to talk. But now the call was connected.

Maylene: Hello
All Maylene could hear was a very hurt wife on the other end of the phone. She was in tears after she found a letter in her husband's pocket that was signed by one of their peers.

Maylene: Hello…she repeated

Sonwa: Oh my gosh, oh my gosh…Sis. I need to talk to you, it's an emergency!

At this point the children were in the vehicle listening to their music with their headsets on. The brief conversation wasn't audible to them and they didn't have any idea of what was going on. They were aware that this female had done Maylene wrong in the past. But she didn't want to reveal any of this to the children. This was grown folk's business. When she buckled up she mentioned to the girls she needed to make a stop. When they arrived at Sonwa's house she mentioned she would be back shortly and they continued to listen to their music. As soon as Maylene walked into Sonwa's door she was greeted by a very heavy and depressive atmosphere that she knew all too well. She took a deep breath and walked into the front room. She was glad she had the children to remain in the car because she didn't know what to expect.

Maylene: Hey Sonwa. I came as soon as I could. Sonwa reached out and grabbed Maylene because she truly needed a friend.

Then Sonwa stepped back a bit so that she could show Maylene the letter that she found. Fortunately, Maylene didn't have to read the full content of the letter as the details were pretty graphic. The note would only remind her that Jack was just as piggish as Sonwa's husband and she didn't want to open that box at that time. She stood with torn sheets of paper. Sonwa wished this meant the facts would disappear. She said originally when she found the letter she put it in the shredder so no one else would know the actions of her husband. This was contrary to the stories she would share with the girls. On some occasions she would compare her relationship to Maylene's and Jack's and say how they had better communication then any of the woman at the table. How did this feel to call the woman who she spoke down to on numerous occasions? Why didn't she call the ones who she referred to as her immediate posse? Where were they now that she needed them? As much as Maylene wanted to share her thoughts out loud she remembered what she was taught about not gloating about someone else's sorrow. But in her mind she thought, see she is reaping exactly what she has sown.

Maylene: Treading lightly Maylene asked Sonwa what was in her hand. Sonwa was clinching something for dear life and had a crazy look on her face. Then all of a sudden she belted out a painful cry. Sonwa held her chest so tight that Maylene was preparing to dial 911. Was Sonwa having a heart attack?

Sonwa: Now sobbing. She whispered…Maylene she's sleeping with my husband. I would have never thought she would do this to me. While I have been by her bedside after her kidney transplant. Can you believe she would be so conniving? The people she expected to support her never showed up. In disbelief she asked Maylene, can you believe this?

Maylene: Buying herself time to answer the question carefully Maylene asked, to whom are you referring?

Sonwa wanted Maylene to give her hope. She wanted to believe her buddy hadn't done what the letter said. The evidence was in her face. But now this was beginning to overtake her. What could she do? Reality had set in. Her girl was making love to her husband right in her bed and bragging about this when they would meet for their girl's days out. It all was coming back to her. She could remember the vivid conversations of how he would kiss her behind her ear and stroke the fine hairs on her neck. How he would nestle up in her arms like he was a kid nursing from their mother's breast. It was her associate's husband she was talking about all along. Sonwa wondered how she missed this affair. Then she got super angry. She screamed like a lion in a jungle. Then she fell to her knees onto the mahogany wood floor. Her whole body shook as if she was having a seizure and then Maylene looked down and under her was a big wet puddle. Sonwa lost control; she hadn't gone to the bathroom for hours. She said she didn't have time to go because she was too angry to sit. But the body does what it wants when it wants and thankfully

Maylene was there to pick up the pieces. She ran to the kitchen to get some paper towels and a glass of water to help clean up the mess. In no time she returned to help her childhood friend. It's funny how the tables will turn when a person is in need. Then there came a point when Maylene seen that Sonwa held something tight in her other hand. May could see it was a feminine garment. So she slowly lifted one of Sonwa's fingers at a time and finally she was able to open her hand fully. There it was a pair of Rhoda's panties that she purchased at Betsy's lingerie party. They were unique in that they had initials branded on the thong. Her panties somehow ended up in Sonwa's husband's laundry basket.

Sonwa: With saddened eyes she said, she basically told me she was making love to my husband all of these years. She was talking about my husband when she said she was carrying a married man's baby. She made it out as if it was a joke but she wasn't playing. In the letter she said her husband was less of a man because he couldn't get her pregnant. Wow....this tramp is piece of work!

Sonwa's plan was to go to the hospital where Rhoda was and assassinate her. Maylene wished that she didn't hear her say this. She didn't want to be a witness or knowledgeable of any crime.

Sonwa: Yes, God doesn't like ugly and I'm going to help him take this girl out. That's why she couldn't carry any of those babies, old cheating behind. Then Sonwa walked to the front door where her sling back shoes sat alongside her tall umbrella. She slipped them on and invited Maylene to go with her to the hospital. Then she threw on her fur coat as if it was the perfect outfit.

Sonwa: I'm going up to that hospital to wrap those IV cords around neck!

Maylene: Oh nooooo, you have way too much going for you to let your life be destroyed further by this sicko! Trust me I know your pain. But believe me she wasn't just sleeping with your husband.

Sonwa stopped suddenly in her tracks. She looked at Maylene. Then she paused for what felt like a while.

Sonwa: Are you saying you knew this fool was sleeping with my husband?

Maylene: I am saying I had an idea when she kept me apart from you and Goisha every time you all had your girl's night out. Then I saw her writing in her journal while I did her hair. She said all kinds of stuff about the numerous men who escorted her to business parties and I knew she wasn't just fantasizing; these stories were for real. And besides I didn't owe you anything after you all treated me so nasty. I came here by mistake. You know how it is when you wave to someone who is going by and you wish you could take your greeting back? But I'm here now and this is what counts.

Whoa, this didn't end well. Have you ever felt like telling someone what you really think?

Maylene walked out of the house with her head up high while feeling as if she had just accomplished one more goal that she didn't realize she had formed in her mind. It was at that time that Maylene began to see people who wronged her in the past began to suffer themselves. Was it God's revenge that she read about as a child? Were her former battles being handled without her help? I guess her grandmother was right. She would always say, just watch and see God will handle it.

CHAPTER 6
JUST WATCH

The unexpected knock on the door came at a perfect time. Maylene wanted out of the conversation with her mother-in-law. Maylene chuckled to herself as she thought maybe this was God's way of changing the subject. However, this was not a laughing matter....

A week later

Maylene walked around the house for hours with a look of concern on her face. She couldn't get real life off of her mind and she had to evaluate what she might have to do next to continue to take care of her elderly mother in law and the minor children. Clearly the big house was unaffordable and she didn't know how she would be able to sustain the enormous bills. Jack did not leave her with the means to handle the remaining expenses. That would have been too easy for him to do. He wanted her to suffer for some reason. Why would a real man want to do this? That question remained unanswered for quite a while but in the mean time she needed to figure out her plan B.

57

As she stood looking at the little food in the frig her mother in law quietly walked over to her as she leaned on her black cane.

Mother Frost: "Daughter can we talk for a minute? I have a lot that I need to say to you. I'm sure you do not want to hear it. But as a mother I want you to give me a chance to make my point. If you don't like what I have to say you can just ignore me like all of my children."

Maylene: feeling very guilty just as Mother Frost intended Maylene agreed to sit down and listen to what Mother had to say. Although she was reluctant she didn't want to appear to be disrespectful.

They both walked back into the living room and sat quietly on the large white leather chairs when Mother Frost noticed a nick in the side of the one she sat in.

Mother Frost: Well I want you to know that I see the havoc that you have been through and how you are trying to do everything on your own. I know that I shouldn't be your responsibility but it doesn't change the fact that I am here with you and not with my own children. As I am sitting here I see someone has put a nick in your leather chair. It better not be those old bad nieces and nephews of yours. I keep trying to tell my grandchildren this is not their home and they better take their bad selves back to their house if they want to mess up somebody's property. Oh, I know I got off subject. I better move my seat so I can stay focused.

She stood up slowly because she was in a lot of pain due to her arthritis. Then she finally reached her seat that was only a few feet away. It was so good that she wanted to live independently.

Mother Frost: So, as I was saying I am not blind. You are having a hard time taking care of all of us and it doesn't make sense that you have to take care of me when I have my own children who should be doing what you are doing. But I want you to know I really do appreciate you taking me in. My son made some very poor decisions although he probably thought they were good decision at the time. But now it's your turn to make these decisions and I want to help you if you will allow me. Please don't let your pride speak for you it will only get in your way. There was a pause and then Mother continues to share her thoughts. Maylene wanted to interrupt her but everything she said was absolutely true.

Mother Frost: Now that I have your full attention I want you to take me to the bank on tomorrow I told my son this day would come. I have a small savings for you and the kids. I want to sign it over to you.

Maylene: You are doing enough. Please do not worry about a thing. Yes, it is very tough right now but it will not always be this way. Mother I do not want your money. I take care of you because of my love for you. And I told myself several years ago that if I am lucky God would send someone to do the same for my mother in the event I am unable. Then she leaned over to give Mother a kiss and to get back to her chores. Then she called her youngest daughter to lend her a hand.

Maylene: Autumnnnnn, please go downstairs and get me the laundry out of the dryer and make sure you close the dryer door. There is some fresh linen inside that I want you to put on your bed and I will come help you in a few minutes. Maylene went into the kitchen to clean out the refrigerator as she did each week before she went to the grocery store. But the truth of the matter was there was not much to clean because they literally were living on less and less. Mother Frost had seen this look before. With her small black cane, she walked over and leaned on the refrigerator door.

Mother Frost: Daughter I would be honored to help. I will definitely be ready first thing in the morning. When she said this she meant 5:00 a.m. when everyone was sleep. Maylene had no intent on getting up that early and besides the store wasn't open. Mother wanted to go to the bank first and probably wanted Maylene to sit in the bank parking lot so they would be the first customers.

Maylene: Mother I may have a small job to do in the morning. I get paid daily so we will be alright. But the truth of the matter was Maylene would be praying for a miracle. If she didn't get it she really didn't know what she was going to do. Then there was a knock on the door. Maylene thought maybe this was God's way of changing the subject. When she opened the door it was the police looking for her adult son.

60

Maylene: Officers he does not live here anymore. He is an adult and he has a family of his own.

Officer 1: Well the last address we have on file is this one. He didn't show up for court. He has an outstanding warrant. It would behoove him to take care of this Mam before it gets worse.

Maylene: I will tell him when I see him although I rarely see him at all. But thank you officers. Have a good night.

Officer 2: You too Mam. But officer 1 appeared to have a suspicious look on his face. Did he see something that they did not? Could Maylene take another episode of tragedy? She had to watch to see.

He Loves Me, He Loves Me Knot, He Loves Me!

CHAPTER 7
TRAGEDY
24 Hours Later

The fire was blazing and you could see the side of the house burning right before your eyes. The neighbors all yelled out to the fireman "PLEASE HELP SIR PLEASE HELP, THERE IS A PREGNANT WOMAN IN THE HOUSE WITH HER FOUR-YEAR-OLD DAUGHTER!

Arie suffered third degree burns from a fire that was said to have resulted from her husband's neglect in handling an electrical problem that he put off for months. One of his friends who was a licensed electrician came over and seen the danger that this issue posed. He warned John to take care of the matter right away. But John continued to tell Arie that there was pressing bills that were a priority and the electrical problem would be taken care of as soon as they could afford it. But this never happened. Instead the house caught fire and John almost came home to a lost family that he would have buried if it wasn't for the neighbor's brother who was visiting on his day off from the fire department. Arie was smiling and humming as she prepared their unborn baby's soon arrival. She was pleased with the chosen design that she found in a home decorating magazine.

Arie: Wow, I did not expect it to come out so beautiful. Thank God for all the nice gifts that our little girl will get to come home to. Elizabeth come see what Mommy did with the picture you painted for your little sister.

Elizabeth didn't come running as she would have normally. Just as Arie was about to call her again she heard someone yelling outside of the nursery window.

Off Duty Fireman:
HELLO, HELLO YOU NEED TO GET OUT OF THE HOUSE! IMMEDIATELY GET OUT OF THE HOUSE!!!

Arie ran to the window to see what the commotion was about. Arie: Sir, what's wrong she asked as she looked down from the second floor?

ODF: THE FRONT OF YOUR HOUSE IS ON FIRE! IS THERE ANYONE ELSE IN THE HOME?

Arie: Yes, my four-year-old daughter.

Arie began to call out for Elizabeth again as she searched for her but she didn't answer. Arie even checked her hiding places but she still couldn't find her. Before you knew it the fire was beginning to grow out of control on the lower level of the home. Arie still could not smell the fire because of her diagnosis but she could see that it was now blazing. She was so panicked that she went into labor. She fell to the floor because of the sudden sharp pains she felt in her abdomen.

She cried out OH GOD PLEASE DON'T LET ME LOSE MY TWO BABIES! PLEASSSE SAVE US GOD......PLEASE. Then she passed out.

Moments later the thick black smoke hovered over the entire house. Right on time the off duty fireman climbed into the nursery window and he began looking for Arie and Elizabeth. As he was looking for them he heard a small cry.

Elizabeth: Mommy come save me. I'm over here.

The officer let the sound of the child lead him to her location. There she was under her bed curled up and terrified.

Officer: I am here to help you sweetheart. Please take my hand. The more he tried to help her, the more fearful she was.

Elizabeth: You are a stranger. Then she started to cough and struggled to breath.

The officer didn't have time to acquaint himself with her and he had to aggressively pull her from under the bed.

He ran to the window in which he came through. There outside the window was his brother and some neighbors who held the ladder that he borrowed from another neighbor. Soon the rescue team arrived to take over where the officer left off. They looked for Arie but at this time she had caught fire.

By the time they got her out everyone thought she would not live. She was taken to the burn center that was close to their home. The unborn baby was delivered but Arie was in a coma for quite some time.

When she finally woke up she was covered with bandages from the third degree burns. It took her a very long time to look at herself because she was fearful of what she might see. She would imagine how terrified her little Lizzy might be when seeing her for the first time after the accident. She knew she had to come to terms with who she was now that she had changed on the outside. How could she expect her daughter to reacquaint herself with her mother if Arie was a stranger to herself?

She had so much to deal with. She was so grateful for her sisters in law who cared for their new baby girl while she recovered. They took turns relieving John so that he could spend time with his wife and to take care of Elizabeth.

The healing time was difficult but eventually Arie was discharged from the hospital and had to learn how to resume living again. Some forewarned her that it would be extremely difficult on the marriage and most definitely difficult for a new way of living. After so much time went by Arie and John decided to separate because of the distance that grew between them. John said he no longer found his wife attractive and he knew this would not change. That was until the fireman who saved his wife's life began to see Arie at many events as it related to victims of fire. He seen past her disfigured face and her mask that she most often wore and he fell in love with her. The people in the city were amazed that such a story like this could happen. They read about such things but now it was in their neighborhood. This began to circulate around town. John realized what he was missing and tried to rekindle their love. It's funny how people can want what is no longer available. Arie filed for a divorce and her ride or die stood by her the whole time. Although Maylene didn't want to see her friend divorce she knew it was time for Arie to move on. Sometimes we have to make drastic decisions when we have been burned by the people we love. **Have you ever been burned?**

He Loves Me, He Loves Me Knot, He Loves Me!

CHAPTER 8
HANDICAP

I lost control of my new BMW and nearly lost my life! I now know what you meant in the past about putting stock in material things. All I have now is this.

Mam can I help you get that? The customer said as Maylene stood in aisle seven trying to get the last yogurt off of the shelve far back in the refrigerator.

But the customer wasn't talking to her; he was talking to the lady in the wheel chair who had a severe accident that prevented her from walking on her own. She was paralyzed from the waist down and she appreciated the young customer asking her if she needed help.

Female Customer: Sunny you are so kind. As a matter of fact, I can use your help. Then she took out her long grocery list that she now expected this young man to gather up since he offered to help. When Maylene heard her voice it prompted her to look over. This voice sounded familiar but the lady did not. She wanted to look closer to see why this person seemed so familiar. But she was taught as a child that it is impolite to stare so she tried hard to find another way to see why she sounded so familiar.

Maylene: Now talking to the woman in the wheelchair. Mam are those juices on sale? Maylene pointed to the juices that were in the lady's basket. They are my favorite. I love that flavor. That brand is excellent!

Female Customer: Yes, they are on sale. There aren't many left. How are you today May-May?

Maylene almost fell into the lady when she realized it was her old childhood friend Peggy. By friend she meant acquaintance. This associate was very mean as a youngster and her attitude did not change for better as she developed. In fact, she got worst. She was very aggressive with her tongue and she had no filter. She took digs at people who were plus size and made it no secret that they were the lowest of God's creation from her perspective. She would put a person on full blast whenever she seen they'd gained a pound, she associated it with being greedy and lazy. It didn't matter if you just gave birth or had other valid reasons for being overweight.

Peggy: Hey give me a hug girl, long time no see! I figured you didn't know it was me. She said with a nervous laugh. I put on a few pounds after my car accident. You see I lost control of my new BMW and nearly lost my life! I now know what you meant in the past about putting stock in material things. All I have now is this. She pointed to her wheelchair that seemed to be on the brink of breaking down. As they stood talking for a bit some mean kids walked by.

Kids: Eeeee.....She is so fat! She must eat like a pig. Then they made pig sounds while their parents went from door to door in the grocery isle. The kids were not disciplined for being disrespectful to this disabled woman.   Then all of a sudden one of the mother's heard Peggy talking and she turned around and took off her glasses. She looked closer and seen that it was Peggy her old schoolmate.

The Parent: Peggy is that you? She said as she chewed on her minty fresh gum. Oh my gosh, chump, chump, chump you really let yourself go!

Peggy looked at Maylene and she didn't need to say a word. Peggy was only getting back what she dished out. Boy did this hurt! It's not that she was only mean as a youth; she was this way towards people who were not in the same financial bracket as herself. God forbid you were a size bigger than a zero. She would talk about you until she brought you to tears. How fast the tables can turn when we aren't careful how we judge. And to make matters worse her husband left her for a plus size woman who he said he loved back in the day but he was afraid of what others would think about him.
Hey curves are in!!!

He Loves Me, He Loves Me Knot, He Loves Me!

CHAPTER 9
TOUGH TIMES

The serene got her attention. Who was in trouble now? Low and behold it was Maylene. She was being pulled over by the police. Yeah, what now?

Six months later....

Girls it's time to get up. Don't want you to miss the bus. Just as she said this Mother Frost looked over at the clock.

Mother Frost: Are you still going to take me to the bank?

Maylene: Mother we already went to the bank. Would you like some breakfast?

Mother: No what I would like is to go live with my daughter.

Maylene: I wish I could help you with this but they aren't able to take you right now.

Mother cried and cried like a baby. Maylene could not get her to stop. She didn't know what to do. Jack promised this wouldn't happen and he left Maylene handling the stress of everything all on her own. Now what should she do. It seemed everything was going wrong. Although she felt God was trying to tell her we reap what we sow she didn't know how much longer she could wait for her harvest to come. She was a giver. She had a heart of love. She never wanted to see others suffer in spite of how they treated her. But God was moving way too slow and she was lonely all the time. One day she said that's it, I have to think about myself. I'm going to doll myself up and take myself out. With what money you might ask? This family was doing badly. Even with the side jobs that she had. She wasn't finding any full time jobs that would offer her mother's hours so she could be home in time to get her daughter off of the school bus because she went to school a couple of miles away from their home. Now digging in the bottom of her special purse she was able to gather up a few dollars that was meant for gas to get around to find a full time job. She figured I can do both. I will spurge on myself and get a gourmet coffee and a Danish. This was the only splurging that she could do. She had to resort to thinking what she wished she had and make believe that it came true.

Maylene: I know that Jack only paid the car insurance for a short period of time. I better get some money soon or I will not be able to drive my car. This time came sooner than later. When Maylene called herself out painting the town at the local mall while her daughter was in school she got pulled over by the local police after she left the mall to go home.

Police Officer: License and registration please.

Maylene: Sure officer she said with confidence as she took out the papers from her glove compartment. Can you tell me why you pulled me over I was just leaving the mall?

Police Officer: Mam I pulled you over because you have a broken tail light.

Maylene: Oh, I didn't realize this. I will take care of this officer. In her mind she thought I could barely buy this Danish and coffee, I know I can't get this light fix right now.

The officer walked away to only return with bad news. Maylene could see this in his face and didn't need to add to her year of chaos.

Police Officer: Mam, do you realize you have no insurance on your car?

Maylene: No officer I wasn't aware of this.

Officer: I will have to ask you to get out of the car Mam. We will tow it to the garage and you will need to show proof of insurance before the vehicle will be released.

Maylene: Sir, this is my only means of transportation.

Police: I'm sorry Mam I'm just doing my job.

He Loves Me, He Loves Me Knot, He Loves Me!

Maylene didn't know what she was going to do. She was so tired of asking people for help. But when all fails as they did for one another, she knew she could call on her ride or die and Arie agreed to pick her up. But Arie had a flat tire and didn't have a spear. Maylene began to panic as the hour was growing near. There was no one home to get Autumn and she was too young to get home on her own.

Arie: Sis I am so sorry. My car broke down. I have a flat. Can you call Rhoda?

Maylene knew desperate times called for desperate measures but she wasn't that desperate. Keeping in mind what many women had gone through much because of this female and her lack of respect. Maylene did not see herself begging this treacherous woman for anything. She stood tall in her wedged heels and said: No thanks. I would rather walk. And this is what she did until her old friend showed up in a nick of time.

G: Well, well we meet again.

Maylene: Yes ….. and with shame she apologized for avoiding his calls and failing to be the friend to him as he was to her.

G: No problem. Why are you walking? Is your car down or something?

Maylene: Unfortunately, it is. She didn't want to get into the details of it all.

G: I have a boy who is a mechanic if you want me to connect you with him.

Maylene: Not right now. I am still looking for full time work.

G: Are you still doing home interior designs?

Maylene: Yes, when the jobs are available.

G: My church has a bulletin board filled with jobs I will see what you might be interested in. As a matter of fact, would you like me to take you over there?

Maylene: My baby will be home soon. I have to get home.

G: No problem. I can take you to get her and then we can go to the church.

Reluctantly Maylene agreed. Why did it seem all eyes were on her when she got out of his car to get Autumn? When she brought Autumn in the car they stopped into the house to drop off her things. Then she took a moment to tell her older daughter where they were going and Summer gave her a look as if she had egg on her face.

Summer: Ummmm, Mama why are you riding with him?

Maylene: Because the police took our car. I will fill you in later but do not tell your grandmother.

77

Too late Mother heard everything. It was funny how she was deaf on some days and could hear A1 on others.

Mother: Daughter who is that in the driveway?
Maylene: A friend of mine
She gave Mother a kiss and told her she would be back soon.

Just as she was leaving Summer said: it would have been nice to know that you were going to start dating.

Maylene: Feeling bad…. but only for a moment she responded to Summer. I am not dating but that does sound like a good idea. Then she smiled.

Summer: Mama just because Daddy left does not mean you have to ruin your life too.

Maylene stood in one place as she looked as if she seen a ghost.

Summer: We all know that Daddy is gone but remember he left us devastated. When the police handed you those divorce papers you fainted to the floor. I witnessed the whole thing and now I'm watching you go through something else with another man. Please Mama be careful. I don't want you to make a name for yourself. Thankfully the church helped us to move on but please do not make us go backwards.

Maylene: Memories began to flood Maylene's mind. Why did Summer have to do this to her as she was leaving out of the door? She couldn't let life overtake her again. Even though divorce is like death she had to move forward as would a widow. The grave clothes had to come off. What better time than in that moment?

He Loves Me, He Loves Me Knot, He Loves Me!

.

CHAPTER 10
WHAT'S NEXT

Maylene was being followed. How creepy was this?

Weeks later…..

Maylene was waking up each day thinking how angry she was that she let Jack treat her so badly for such a long time. She began to think of the days she contemplated revenge while they were still together. Like the day she sat in her car looking up the people who propositioned her from time to time. For example, his so called friends, his boys. How would he like it if she took them up on their offer? They whispered, you are too good for this dude, dump him! At first she felt defensive but she knew she couldn't react. The phone conversations went on for a short while before Maylene no longer felt guilty about having male friends and she didn't feel a need to be loyal to Jack any longer. She began to return calls to his fellow coworkers who gave her the skinny on her cheating husband. But what Maylene learned later was Jack was having her followed. He even involved their son and Jr. reported to him what he believed he seen. This infuriated Maylene. But what they seen is what they got for being nosey. Smile.

But this attitude didn't last long. Maylene became concerned when she was told that Jack had plans to kill her new male associates.

81

Isn't it odd that a man who has cheated for decades with countless woman would feel he had a right to be angry with his soon to be ex-wife?

Deception has a way of destroying relationships and families. What are your thoughts about deception?

CHAPTER 11

DATING

Squirt, squirt was the sound of Maylene's perfume as it permeated the room. She imagined her favorite fragrance would follow him home once their evening was over. It would be a reminder to him that this woman found him to be very charming and she made it no secret that she was very interested in him. He gave her the attention that she wanted and she could imagine this relationship going in a good direction.

Maylene felt beautiful as she hummed and pranced around in the cold bedroom. She was bringing a little sunshine into her own life even if it was at the expense of losing a battle and hoping to win a war.

Maylene: Thinking to herself, I wonder if he would like this dress or that one, considering the burnt orange goes better with my complexion. I'm thinking this would be the better of the two. Utt oh, there's a stain. Ok, that one is out and my little black freekum dress is in. Smile. Whallah!!!! Like a magic wand, she waved her hand back and forth. Ting was the sound of perfection! It was like the approval of a rare diamond. Maylene's eyes glistened as she became more excited about her night out. Then Maylene went to her walk in closet to find the perfect pump. This wasn't an easy decision. She loved the variety of shoes that she owned. Which one would give her the look she wanted? Hmmmm, then one finally jumped out at her. They were her favorite shoes once upon a time. The ones she wore when she and Jack would paint the town or go to special events. Memories flooded her mind. Maylene was giving herself whiplash. She was almost as bad as Jack. The emotional going back and forth really wasn't healthy. But these were the good times. The times when they laughed and laughed. Their hearts were content and they wanted the world to know about it. Maylene held the shoe in her hand as she reminisced about a church event. During this time the minister asked the congregation to look at their neighbor and to ask them "Aren't you happy you came?" So they did exactly that. When they looked at one another Jack gave Maylene a look that said you have something on your face. The problem was he spoke as the old Chinese movies did when the character and the words spoken never lined up. It was even harder to follow what Jack was attempting to say when his lips and words were on separate pages. This caused Maylene to take out her compact mirror and she soon found it was her false lashes that Jack was trying to warn her about. After crying in service after the worship songs the lash adhesive began to lift. Jack said at first the loose lashes looked like a spider. Thank God they figured it out or Jack could have run into traffic trying to get away from her. He was a bugaphobe. They laughed and laughed until they almost had to leave the sanctuary. Boy was that funny. A memory that Maylene didn't mind recapping. But she decided they were not the best choice for her night out because she didn't want to think about Jack while she was out on the town with another man. So she put the shoes back in her closet. Then she located another pair. They seemed to be the ones. Then she looked for the matching leather bag that she brought together with the shoes. It was so far in the back of her closet that she could barely reach it. Then her daughter Summer came knocking at the door.

Summer: Mama…. she sung in her cheerful voice…where are you?

Maylene: I'm in here!

Summer: Where is here? Then she chuckled. Oh, here you are Mum!!! When she found her mother she seen the host of shoes, dresses and other artifacts that her father had gifted Mrs. Frost several years prior. Maylene didn't let her go too far.

She could see the twinkle in Summer's eyes. She was like a kid in the candy store. Her daughter was having a hard time keeping her hands off of the items that were in the don't touch zone. Then she began to visit some of her favorites in the areas that was permitted to be perused.

Summer: Remember this Mama? You use to love this dress like crazy. Boy it has been years huh?

Maylene: Yes it has.

Summer: I'm glad you are giving the resurrected Daddy another chance, she giggled.   Your new man, she said as she sashayed in the dressing space.

Maylene: Looking at Summer with a frown. Daughter are you ok?

Summer: Yes, I'm ok. Why do you ask?

Maylene: What would make you think I am going out with your dad?

Summer: Brother said Dad came by and you two were going to give it another chance.

Maylene: That's a negative not an affirmative.

Summer: Looking a little disappointed. Hmmmm.....I wonder why brother would say this unless he thought it was true.

Maylene moved on to get herself ready for her date. After she was finished she liked what she seen. Soon her date arrived and low and behold Maylene noticed Jack hiding in the trenches. He couldn't fool her. She knew this man like a book. It would have been more surprising to not see him than to see him at all. Jack had a reputation that preceded him. Apparently Summer peeped him hiding as well. She couldn't wait to tell her mother privately and she would have the opportunity shortly after they left. Summer waited a brief moment and then she called her mother's cellular phone.

Summer: Mama I believe I seen Daddy's car follow you and your friend down the street. I hope you don't mind but I called brother and told him what I think I seen. Mama, Daddy has been following you for weeks? Brother said he even put him on the case.

Maylene: Not wanting to alert her date she gave Summer coded answers. When she got off of the line he asked her is everything ok.

Maylene: Sure. How close are we to the restaurant?

Home Boy: Ummm not that far.

He was correct. They soon arrived at the upscale restaurant where she was treated like royalty. The servers did everything but spoon feed her. She looked around the room and seen nothing but class. Then her phone buzzed. She put it on vibrate before they entered the restaurant. She was glad she did.

Summer: Sorry to bother you Mom but Clyde and Jr. said Dad plans on taking your friend out! Should I report this to the police?

She was panicked. This wasn't something they should take lightly. Everyone knew Jack could be a little over the top and get back up from one of his closest friends. His name was "The Revolver." He kept it in his holster and made many people nervous because he wore it as a lady would her feminine accessories.

Maylene: Can you excuse me for a minute; I need to use the powder room. As she stood the wait staff rushed to help her and escorted her to the lady's room. It was there that she whispered to Summer that she probably wouldn't be able to talk further until her date was over. She told her daughter calling the police didn't sound like a good option. She planned on finishing her night out and she would pray nothing happened as Jack allegedly premeditated. Then they ended their call. At this point Maylene noticed a familiar face looking back at her. It seemed as if she was ease dropping. Maylene wasn't sure if she was just paranoid or was she a spy for Jack? She knew from that point on to be on her guard.

Isn't it odd that a cheating man of decades feel he has a right to kill someone who has an interest in his wife who he

has abandoned? Sure she was still his wife by law...but what about the marital vows?

He Loves Me, He Loves Me Knot, He Loves Me!

CHAPTER 12

BACK AGAINST THE WALL

Mrs. Tampa: Mrs. Frost you need to come home quick! Summer locked herself out of the house and Mrs. Tuity seen her going back and forth to the side of the house to go pee-pee. She said she looked for an adult but the only person she thought she seen was your elderly mother-in-law. She said she rang the bell but no one answered.

Maylene woke up the next day, recapping many of her past encounters. Realizing old times could bring up old feelings, some good and some bad. Her dear friend Manny aka G told her this happens to many people who have lost a love one. They could have feelings of guilt and be emotionally all over the place. A grieving person can wonder if they would ever love again. Then at times one may be angry because the mate has left and they are all alone. He said if these emotions were not handled correctly it could be a problem. So Maylene decided to go sit in her car where she could emote without reservations. If she decided she wanted to scream or cry she could do this and not worry about her children hearing her. She didn't want to leave in their young minds the question is our mother losing hers? She knew that she didn't live in a perfect world. The closest she would get to it being perfect was that the fairy tale story never ended. But this wasn't healthy and she decided she would take G's suggestion to go and get grief counseling for her lost so she could move forward with her life. She began to see a minister from a sister church who was a much respected leader. He complimented Maylene several times in the session. She felt his words were genuine while in the same very appropriate. They read many scriptures and scheduled her for a few group sessions. Unfortunately, his secretary didn't think this was necessary and she made it no secret. One day she approached her and forbid her to come again. One of the mothers of the church overheard her threat and she addressed the sister in front of Maylene. This was all good but she decided to cut her ties. The lessons that she got from the minister and the others around him was enough for her to get herself back in church and from there some things began to turn around. That was until the rumors got started that Maylene was seeing her lover that she had before she and Jack separated. A very tough pill to swallow for a woman who never thought it would be her. She had to deal with more folks talking and more gossip brewing. She would go to one of her confidants whose name was Ronee and she had patients of a saint. She advised Maylene to listen to the voice of God until she had a huge spat with her husband who was a musician in the church. Unfortunately, she didn't have the best words to relay to her friend from that point on. Her very own marriage could use some intervention to say the least. They agreed to keep one another in prayer

It can be difficult to encourage someone when you are going through a storm. But it is important to have someone you can depend on that has your best interest.

Ronee: Sis, I was thinking it would be nice if you and the kids could come over for dinner next week. How does Thursday at six sound to you?

Maylene: Sounds good, we will see you then.

By this time this invite was needed. The food in their house had grown to nothing and Maylene's mother in law was becoming more than she could handle financially. Maylene didn't dare take her mother in law's offer to contribute to the house. She didn't want anyone to every think she would take advantage of her. But she had to break the news to her soon to be former husband.

Maylene: Jack, you have to find somewhere else for your mother to go.

It was as if the dead had come alive. He didn't have anything to do with his former family. This included Maylene or his children. He claimed it was because of his new fiancée. He said she didn't like children and this part of his life was over. What was odd about this was his fiancée had children of her own. Was this an excuse of Jack's to keep them apart or was it

93

a fact? If it was true neither of them took into account that he left many unresolved issues and Maylene wasn't going to let him stay in the coffin while she stressed to make ends meet. She certainly wasn't going to sell her soul to get men to pay her bills. Why should she have to do this when Jack claimed to be the man of the house. Real men do not leave their families stranded after they tell their wives they want them to be stay at home house wives.

Maylene: Jack, I think enough time has passed that we will need to address some pertinent issues. I am taking you to court for alimony and child support because we do not deserve to live like pheasants. You do not get a free go card and a window blind to block us out. I am glad that you have moved on but you still have obligations over here.

Jack: I am in love with my new fiancée and I owe her everything I got. You need to find a job and take care of yourself. You are no longer my responsibility.

Maylene: Believe me I do not want to deal with you at all. I just want you to know that I will not tolerate this any further even if it means I will be humiliated in front of a crowded court room of strangers who will hear our dirty laundry. By the way did you get the letter that I wrote to you and your mistress, I mean fiancée? I included her since I expect she will eventually be in our daughter's life. That is on the days that she has true visitation with you and not a do drop in. it speaks to the needs of our child and that she needs to be with you some weekends so I can have a break.

Jack: A break? You have to be kidding.

Maylene: YES, A BREAK! I deserve to move on with my life as well. You never keep your scheduled visits without you hearing my mouth. Don't forget you was so adamant about one more child. She is BOTH of our responsibility. Thank God we drafted a contract because you always play the I got Amnesia game. But I'm calling you on the carpet. This is one matter I will not let you sleep away.

Jack: What are you talking about?

Maylene: I'm talking about consistency. I also need your help with the expenses of before and after care for our child.

Jack: WHAT? ARE YOU CRAZY???? She is old enough to let herself in the house. I am not paying for a baby sitter.

Maylene: Maybe your wife might have a little sympathy considering I hear she has children of her own. Would she let her young child be responsible for themselves at such a young age?

Jack: Ask her for yourself.

Then his fiancée made her presence known.

Maylene had to look past the fact that this was the female he cheated with. She had to get along with the female who would play an intricate role in their child's life. Their daughter's care was certainly much more important than discussing his infidelity.

The future Mrs. Frost 2: Maylene, I have been on the line the whole time. No, we will not pay for her childcare. She should be able to let herself into the house.

Maylene tried to explain the dangers of this suggestion. Neither of them would listen and the conversation ended badly. Weeks later Maylene found a job. She interviewed for numerous positions but finally one came through. She knew she had no one to take care of Autumn so she began to teach her how to let herself into the house. That was until she got an emergency call from her elderly neighbor who said Autumn was found sitting in Maylene's parked car in the driveway. Autumn lost her key at school. She tried to hide from the neighbor because she knew her mother would get in trouble. She was right the police and social services were at the door waiting for her when she rushed home. They warned her that she ran the risk of losing her child if this should ever happen again. The law could recognize this matter as extreme neglect. On the next day Maylene wrestled with the fact that she would have to quit her job. She needed the money badly and she had no one who could be dependable enough to help her get Autumn safely from the bus stop to the house. But she didn't need to worry about quitting the job any further. When she arrived to her classroom with her daughter to start her day with her students the program director called her into the office and regretfully had to fire her. She reminded her that she left her own students to pick up her child and left the numerous students with her assistant who was not qualified to be with the children alone. She said she understood she was in a bind and as a mother she may have done the same thing. But Maylene's back was up against the wall. **What do you do when your back is against the wall?**

He Loves Me, He Loves Me Knot, He Loves Me!

CHAPTER 13
NEED ASSISTANCE

Lady don't mess with me. I am not your average client. I'm just as crazy as you. Don't mess with me.

The Next Day

Maylene: Good morning, I was told to fill out an application for food stamps. Am I at the right desk?

Receptionist: Apparently you are since the applications are right in your face.

Maylene kept her comments to herself. She needed assistance and that was the bottom line. But why do people treat others like they are not human? In some cases, there are animals who receive better treatment. While Maylene was filling out the application another applicant noticed she had on a diamond ring.

Applicant: Mam if I were you I would take that ring off. They judge you for everything.

Maylene: Thank you but I think I'm going to keep it on. It is not any of their business what I wear. It is not going to provide what my family and I need right now.

Applicant: Well, I am just saying. They told me I should pawn my jewelry when I originally applied for assistance.

Maylene: I do not know if this is legal. I would check with a manager if I were you.

Applicant: The manager was the person who told me this. She barely let me speak before she began pouncing all over me.

Maylene: It is so sad how people think they can treat the applicants just any old kind of way. I am not going to let them bully me. Then Maylene's name was called. The other individuals in the room were quite angry.

Applicant 3: I have been sitting in this god forsaken place for hours. Who does she think she is to get called before me?

Others began to moan and complain. They agreed that Maylene needed to be at the end of the line because she was the last to be seated. There was people of all types, tall, short, black, white, Asian, thin, plus size and so much more. To look at them they were just like Maylene. Simply put, unemployed. But to hear the crew of community judges aka some government employees, you would think they were supposed to be disheveled and out of control. But these remarks came from those who hadn't been in their shoes. They were the naysayers who judged others as they remarked "Not Me." But no one knows the day nor the hour when trials will strike and call your name. And get this, sometimes these people caused individuals and families to not apply for services because they thought it would be better that they keep their dignity. While others had absolutely no choice. Their pride was set aside in order to put food on the table.

Social Worker: MAYLENE FROST she called a second time.

Maylene could barely see around the partition that was in between her and the social worker. She hoped she wouldn't lose her place while trying to locate the voice that she heard at a distance. She whispered timidly…..

Maylene: Did someone call my name?

Reception: UMM YEAH! It was Mrs. Cap. She is over there. Then the receptionist looked over her bifocal glasses. Can't you see?

Applicant 17: Mam, why did her number get called before the rest of ours? As she held up her ticket that reflected the number seventeen.

The receptionist looked over her glasses and told the applicant to mind her own business.

Applicant 17: I will when you answer my question.

Receptionist: If you want your number to be called at all you better go and sit down someplace.

Applicant 17: Oh, so we are just a number is what you are saying and you do not feel you have to answer my question?

Receptionist: That's right. Don't make me have to put you out!

Applicant 17: Took out her cell phone. Lady I am recording this conversation, I thought you would like to know. Who is your supervisor? I need to speak with a manager.

The receptionist's whole attitude changed.

Receptionist: In a pleasant voice she asked, what did you say your name was again?

Applicant 17: Applicant 17 is what you called me. Feeling fed up she asked the receptionist again, who did you say is your supervisor or manager?

Receptionist: Um, I am going to see where you are on the list and let my supervisor Cori know that we are backed up in here. Sorry for being so cranky towards you I have a toothache and I should have stayed my behind at home. Then she chuckled with a nervous laugh as she held the side of her face. I really shouldn't have taken it out on you.

By the time Applicant 17 came out they were referring to her by her rightful name, Ms. Evergrenate that is.

In the meantime, Maylene was approved for food stamps after arguing with the case worker. He put the wrong code in the system that automatically denied her the benefits that she deserved. She recalled distributing unemployment benefits to her clients many decades prior. And she knew there were still workers who refused to do their job, like her very own caseworker. If she hadn't argued her point she would have left feeling discouraged. But instead she was grateful that the supervisor corrected his error and Maylene didn't have to worry any longer.

Be careful how you treat others your job could be someone else's if you are not careful! Would you agree?

He Loves Me, He Loves Me Knot, He Loves Me!

CHAPTER 14
A JOB

Feeling rejected

Months went by and Maylene continued to work on and off jobs. She was so discouraged that there were many employment vacancies advertised yet she was not getting the positions. What did she have to do to get a full time job? She was timely in providing her resume and she even sent follow up correspondence to express her sincere interest. She had borrowed from Peter to pay Paul until there was no one left to ask for help or at least this is how she felt. Then there was her new Bestie. His name was Mr. Bottle. She said he kept her calm and he did not judge. So she visited him periodically until his coworker introduced himself and offered her to join him for a drink after work. She was extremely apprehensive and she declined his offers every time. Until finally she accepted the invite and she learned he was very kind.

Stranger: So my dear, I have seen you here at the package store maybe a time or two. You're always smiling but what hides behind that smile?

Maylene: Most times I am smiling because I am seeing matters that are worse than my own. But every now and again I may be laughing to keep from crying.

Stranger: Yes, I knew it. I just wanted you to tell your story. Then he chuckled. I'm a pro at this. I can see who you are before a person tells me! Not to put you out there but I have seen your kind before. Most people who come to my second job are stressed, hurting or both. But know that you are not alone, believe me. I have my share of problems too.

This broke the ice between them. Then they went out a few times for drinks at a local restaurant. Wine was fine at first then came the Grand Marnier. Maylene felt guilty because she hadn't drank for over twenty years. But the Grand Marnier felt delicious going down. It was a temporary fix. Over time Maylene's new friend got her a job with the company he worked for in the day. They loved Maylene and so did her new bow, Mr. Clinton. He spoiled her as if she was the best thing that ever happen to him. Within months he brought her a new five speed sports car that she drove around town like a pro racecar driver. Until his maid learned he was in a relationship and maybe in a permanent one at that. She began to do everything to sabotage their relationship. She even planted things in his house and told him it was Maylene's youngest daughter's doing. After a while he began to believe what she said. She had full control over him and he chose to be deflective and not take responsibility when he should. He made it clear that the maid ran the show and he barely spoke with Maylene at one point because the maid threatened to kill them both. He never defended Maylene's honor and this was all she needed to see to know that he was not the one. Later she learned that he didn't want to be alone. They knew they could not live together unless they were married. Maylene wanted to set a good example for her minor daughter. So when Maylene seen this wasn't going anywhere she started dating online where she met numerous men. She interviewed 90 in total in a public restaurant. She was there so frequently that the servers said the establishment was her office. They gave her, her own personal table each time. Until one day the manager got up enough nerve to ask her why such an attractive woman would need to see so many guys. Maylene's response was I have a young daughter at home. I think it would be safer to get to know them in a public place. When you see me with a new person it is because I have learned the previous guy who I met at the restaurant wasn't the one for me. However, the people you seen for a period of time were definite prospects that looked promising. But to my surprise some of them had some good qualities but we were not compatible.

Manager: I see, I see, we were thinking about adding you to our role. Glad to know a little about you my dear then he chuckled and left to help other customers.

Maylene wasn't too sure if she should be embarrassed or keep to her plan of action. Never the less the story went on and she met some very interesting people. Such as a doctor, a judge, a few social workers, a local meteorologist, a news reporter, some successful business owners, and a few accountants. In her eyes they were not the one and she was growing more and more discouraged.

Is there such a thing as the right man? Did he exist? She asked herself was her standards too high?

Maylene: Who am I? I use to be pretty humble years ago. Now I feel no one is right for me. God I'm tired of being lonely even when I have company.

But one thing she knew for sure is that she didn't want to settle. She was a good woman and she deserved a good man. She had faith on some days that man would one day come. He would love her like she had never been loved before and she would honor him in return. But on other days she didn't see this day coming. She tried to not think negative too often because it took away her energy to live. However, there were some thoughts she couldn't escape. Like the upcoming court date and the unresolved matters between her and her soon to be former husband. When they arrived at the court it had been a long time since they'd seen one another. Immediately he made her heart skip a beat. It was as if he rose from the dead. Did she still love this man? How could she still love someone who couldn't love her the way that she felt she should be treated? Then her thoughts were interrupted.

Court Officer: ALL RISE, COURT IS IN SESSION.

The judge scanned the room. He heard many cases. He had a hard job. He had to make some final decisions for couples who couldn't quite make these decisions for themselves. The clerk called the couples one by one. Finally, it was the Frost's turn. They were allowed to speak one at a time. Jack was ready. He chewed on the inside of his mouth in anticipation.

Jack: Good afternoon Your Honor, she is trying to take everything I have and still trying to rule my life. I give her what she needs for my daughters and I do not feel I need to give her another nickel.

Judge: Mrs. Frost how do you feel about what your husband has said?

Maylene: All due respect your honor he and I are legally separated. Ms. Frost is fine.

Judge: According to this motion you two are here regarding your alimony, child support and the overall divorce. In that, I will decide if I will grant the divorce and what your alimony and child support will be. If you didn't notice, I took all the couples before you because I can see you two are still in love. I noticed your eye contact and reactions in comparison to the other couples who apparently were worse off than you two. Sir, in your own words why did you file for divorce?

Jack: She asked me to and eventually I did. I tried to work it out with her but she was being unreasonable. All we did was argue. Then he got choked up.

Maylene: Your Honor may I speak?

Judge: Yes, you may.

Maylene: To be honest I wanted him to be the bad guy before

God. I didn't want to be responsible for pulling the plug.
Maylene couldn't hold back her emotions. The truth of the
matter is he tried to delay the divorce but I kept pushing for
him to file. My mother-in-law warned us about the pain that
came with both of our problems. Me being too bull headed
and not flexible and him being a cheater. But we didn't listen.
We were both too angry at times and didn't think rationally
and we held on to too many bad memories. But I only thought
about myself at the time because I have always put so many
people before me. I wanted out without a penalty attached. I
thought if he filed I would escape the wrath of The Lord. He
was the only one I was concerned about. Your Honor I don't
want to put all of this on Jack because he did come back home
with all of his things. But when he told me he escaped his
mistress while she was at work it made me angry all over
again. So I rejected him. The same way I felt that he rejected
me. On top of it all he asked if I would allow him one more
night out so he could close the relationship officially. I guess
what I am saying is we both are at fault. I wish things weren't
so bad but he is right we do not see eye to eye any longer.

Judge: Well Mr. and Mrs. Frost, I have seen couples for many,
many years and you two are a unique case. He has written
down some pretty nice things about you and you seem to be
defending him as well. You didn't get to thirty years together
by accident. You have been a good provider and by your own
testimony she has done a phenomenal job with your family as
a stay at home wife. At this time Maylene was covered in
tears. The judge made them both look at some of their best
times together. Aside from the infidelity Jack was a good man
who had a weakness that he never overcame. He loved

Maylene the best way he knew how. He grew up believing LOVE was found in THINGS and not in people. He realized the family needed more than a provider, they needed their Dad and Maylene needed her husband. The image of him continuously cheating on her, one woman after another, was one memory she wanted to put to rest.

Maylene had her own bag of issues that called for professional counseling. If she didn't let go of the past hurt she would continue to be inflexible and the wall of protection would be unbearable in her future relationships. The judge made some great points and denied their request for a divorce and told them to take some time to rethink the whole matter and return in three months. He would review the case when they returned and make a final decision at that time. When the time came months later there was no change and the divorce became final. It was like death that had an indescribable sting. As much as Maylene tried to prepare herself for the day to come this was impossible because she had never been without the man she loved for many decades and the lost was very impacting as it would be for a person who lost an organ. As a result of this unimaginable pain Maylene warned others who contemplated divorce so they didn't have to suffer as she and Jack did. **Death is not easy no matter what form that it comes. Divorce should only be a final resort. Tell us what are your thoughts about divorce?**

He Loves Me, He Loves Me Knot, He Loves Me!

CHAPTER 15
WHIPLASH 91

Who can you trust with your heart? Love can be confusing. One day up and one day down, one day hot, one day cold, is there anyone who is worthy?

One day after life slowed down Maylene and Autumn was at the grocery store making a few small purchases. It felt so good to go to the store to pick up some of the items that they wanted and needed. Maylene opened her small note book that read: 1 bag of Caesar salad, 1 can of tuna, 1 loaf of bread, a quart of milk and one dozen of eggs. Then she seen a reminder at the bottom of her list. It said do not forget Autumn's surprise for being such a good girl. Autumn noticed what her mother wrote on her note pad.

Autumn: Mama thank you for getting my new magazine.

Maylene: Looking surprised. Did you read my note little girl?

Autumn: Yes, Mama, my teacher said we should try reading as often as we can so I have been sounding out the bigger words I see around the house. This way I will be able to read the bigger words in our new school books and Mrs. Lakee gives us prizes for trying hard. Mama are you proud of me?

113

Maylene: Yes, I am proud of you for working so hard. Keep up the good work!

This kept Maylene from responding as she would have because she didn't want Autumn to feel like her teacher told her to do something wrong. At the right time she would talk to Autumn but she didn't want to spoil their little outing at the store. Then Autumn revealed another list that she read.

Autumn: Mama, I could even read your note that you left on the counter! Remember all those names on your paper? I read all 90 of them!

She was so excited. Maylene didn't want to burst her bubble. This was one list she had no business reading. What would people think if Autumn told them how many male friends that she thought her mother had? Was this as important as it was to teach her daughter about boundaries? Was she reading into this way too much? How should she handle it?

Maylene: Buttercup, sweet dumpling, Mommy is very happy that you are such a great reader but you need to get permission before reading someone else's belongings.

Autumn knew this firm tone behind all of the nick names that her mother called her because she hoped it would soften the blow. However, she was very serious and she didn't think this was cute at all. She had to teach Autumn to respect a person's privacy and just as she was about to tell Autumn what would

114

happen if she did this again her old friend Manny aka G came around the corner. He was so happy to see Maylene. They embraced and just as they did Autumn whispered number 91!

Maylene knew her little girl was adding him to the list that she wasn't supposed to read. She gave Autumn the evil eye that said I am going to get you when we get home.

Manny was shopping for one of the mothers of the church who was ill and had several items in his basket.

Autumn remembered Manny from a church service and she recalled her parents arguing about him. Jack said he was way too friendly and he only wanted to take her away from him. Autumn also remembered he was around a lot after Jack was gone and he seemed to always come at the right time. Was he stocking her mother or was this fate? Mother Watkins didn't think so. She said he was a gigolo and the wives who had secret crushes on him were fools. She said they all would have to answer to God one day because they sinned in their minds. She said this also about Maylene and she wasn't taking it back.

Manny: So, how have you been? Longtime no see!

Maylene: Things are starting to look up I think. Fingers crossed. Then she chuckled.

They talked and talked until Autumn slid down on the floor and took a load off. She didn't know how much longer they

115

would talk so she pulled out her little book that she had in her pocket. Maylene and Manny shared about the goings on in their lives and before you knew it they were scheduling time to go out. When they finally met up they reconnected as if they were always together. It didn't matter how long they were apart. Maylene was convinced that bumping into the love of her life from childhood was not a coincidence. How could someone who was rejected by May so many times still have love for her? G said he could never stop loving her. She was born to be his from the start. As months passed they recapped memories that brought about tears. However, Manny promised Maylene the tears she would cry going forward would be better than the tears she cried in her past. What did he mean by this? Well, his actions answered the question. She was his love and priority. He gave May and her girls his very best. He constantly reminded her although they looked to be apart for a long while he never stopped loving her and he made it his business to keep up with the goings on in her life.

Maylene: What #91?????
She said with a big smile. Let me find out you were stocking me! I am going to call you my stocker love. LOL! Did she give him this pet name after she almost disciplined Autumn from calling him this?

G: Well if it means I have my eye on you I guess I am Stocker 91 and on that note he knelt down and asked her if she would be his bride.

116

Maylene said yes immediately! She promised herself she wouldn't let this great guy get away from her again. She promised herself she wouldn't teeter totter if the opportunity presented itself. Was she able to keep her word? It was difficult because of her fear to trust or commit again. She found herself locked up in her emotional roller coaster that soon caused her avoidable whiplash. She imagined an invisible brace around her neck to keep her from reinjuring herself. Because of this invisible brace she allowed herself to be healed emotionally. Soon they began to plan to get married in the Spring and the wedding would be a memorable time in their lives. In the meantime, he began to help her pursue her dreams of being a renown interior designer who would help other woman become entrepreneurs once she was in a financial position to assist them. He worked tirelessly to find the best location in which he felt would fit her visions. Although his schedule was tight, because he coached young men almost every day of the week, he still found time to be there for her and the children. Like the families of his teams the Frost family was blessed. He was known to go beyond his call of duty and not just be a part of the payroll. But he and Maylene missed each other when they were apart. Especially on the weekends when she and her ride or die went on road trips.

He Loves Me, He Loves Me Knot, He Loves Me!

CHAPTER 16
ROAD TRIP

I am lost......

Most of us have experienced being lost at one or more times in our lives. It feels good when we have someone who cares enough to point us in the right directions.

Beep beep beep!!!
Autumn: Mama it's Auntie, can I go get in the car?

Maylene: Yes, just bring the basket we packed and your blanket.

Autumn: Ok, Mama and she did just that. Within moments they were on the road and laughing and having a good old time.

Arie: Sis it's so nice out here today. I think I am going to take off my mask.

This was big for her. She was still very self-conscious of how she appeared to everyone else. But she decided this was the day. The day that she would began to be the woman that was more than the designer mask. The children were in shock but this didn't matter. It was the season for change and Maylene was so proud of her girl. Then Arie stopped the car and said anyone who has to go to the restroom go now. I don't know when we will find a safe place to stop at again. Arie stayed in the vehicle and Maylene escorted the children. She understood Arie wasn't quite ready to go around a bunch of folks but taking the mask off in the car was a start. Then they walked into the building that they soon learned was a church. But as they explored the first floor to find the rest room they seen it was more than that. There stood a group of woman all dressed in red. They were dressed to the T with fine suits and very extraordinary church hats. Some would say they knew who they were. The place was BEAUTIFUL! The interior design was right up Maylene's alley. She was so distracted. Now, Autumn and Elizabeth were dancing in place. They asked if they could try to find the restroom on their own. Maylene was so drawn by the beauty and all of the activities going on that she stopped to talk to people just to see who designed the building and the beautiful interior.

STAFF: Mam the designer is somewhere in the building. I'm not too sure where. I'm told her office is upstairs. Maylene began to look around the oversize room that was made to feel extraordinary yet welcoming. So at this point the girls knew they needed to keep a look out for the restroom. Maylene no longer had to go and she seemed to have forgotten her bestie was out in the car waiting for them. When they got to the second landing Maylene noticed the girls had spotted the bathroom. But now they were no longer the only children with her, now there was three.

Maylene: Autumn and Elizabeth where did that little boy come from and where is his mother? They both looked as if they wondered why she was asking them. Maylene stopped and bent down closer to the little fella's face.

Maylene: Hi little fella. What is your name?

The Little Boy: I am lost.

Maylene: Awww, you are so adorable.
I will bring you to the Pastor or a church officer ok?

The Little Boy: With sad eyes he said…I need the Director.

Maylene: Director? Wow, you're very smart little fella!

The Little Boy: Yes, Mommy said if I ever get lost like my friend Oscar I should go to the Director's office. The director is also the Pastor.

Maylene wasn't sure if this little boy knew what he was saying but she believed they were going in the right direction. So they continued to climb the stairs until they were on the top floor. Whooooo she was blown away. There was furniture that was indescribable. Then a worker came out and she got his attention.

Maylene: Sir this little boy seems to be lost. As she was saying this the girls came from using the restroom. Then the fella told her the way to the Director's office was straight ahead. As they were walking there were some beautiful red sheer curtains blowing lightly in front of three dark wood doors. She didn't know which of the doors was the Director's so she walked closer to see if there was signage. Maylene was so in love with interior design and the joy that it bought others. She wished she could find the director before she burst! Then there was one door slightly ajar. She began to call out, Hello, I'm looking for the Director and the interior designer. Then she heard a strong male voice behind her and he said turn around she's behind you. When Maylene turned around there stood a mirror. All she could see was her own reflection. The male that she heard was nowhere to be found. She began to cry......WOW,WOW,WOW!

Autumn and Elizabeth decided to take the little boy back to the first level. When they did the parents of the little boy were there waiting for him. Maylene was afraid to tell anyone what she experienced until she walked out of the door and there was the love of her life.

SURPRISE! THIS IS ALL FOR YOU!

Maylene was in awe and did not know what to say.

Arie jumped out of the car and ran to her friend with super excitement. Sorry Sis, I knew but I couldn't tell you! Did you see some of your designs in the rooms? We replicated them from some of your portfolios.

Arie grabbed Maylene and hugged her so tight! As she did this she whispered......Sis I knew your blessings were coming and I am so happy for you!!! Now this is what I call real love. Big smiles.

He Loves Me, He Loves Me Knot, He Loves Me!

CHAPTER 17

Thank you

He always had her best interest as well as her family. She prayed for this but she didn't think the day would come. But it did.

The next day Maylene went to church to tell God thank you. Now she felt guilty about being so angry with him periodically. He was so gracious to her and her family. She couldn't thank him enough. She was blessed to have Gentleman back into her life. Not just because of his gift giving but because of his genuine love. She didn't have to question whether it was authentic. He did not waiver and give her whiplash. He didn't leave room for her to doubt why he wanted her as his bride.

He always had her best interest as well as her family's. She prayed for this but she didn't think the day would come. But it did. **What do you do when your prayers have been answered? Do you ask what's next? Do you pick up another worry to fill the void of the last concern?** Well Maylene replaced her former thoughts with a new question. I.e. **How do you deal with the matters of becoming successful? Maylene wasn't worried about failing but rather succeeding.** Would she be able to handle the huge

125

blessing she received unexpectedly? Could she fulfill her dreams? Would she be the successful business woman that she aspired to be? She inherited great qualities from her mother who was wise, intelligent and a highly sought after woman of vigor. With this in mind Maylene began to feel confident that with time she would reach her goals. But after overcoming one fear she adopted another. She soon asked herself repeatedly, "Do we really think we can survive a healthy and successful relationship?" She needed reassurance after all her years of insecurities. How do you know when things are actually working for you as oppose to it being your imagination? When G seen that Maylene was struggling with this he began to coach her just as he did his team players. He explained his methods for building a team was to help them BELIEVE that it was possible. Upon that he would build on specific strategies and important time tables as he got to know each of his team players. He would take note especially in their strengths rather than their weaknesses. He would create a play list of how to undergo the future games. During this time, he would build a confidence in them with ongoing communication and well planned out schedules. The practices were crucial to their bottom line. If they could dedicate themselves to being totally committed they could expect a brighter future. Sure some would need more attention than others but he would make them know that they could depend on him. This rule did not just apply only during the sport season but also in their everyday lives. He taught them that family matters no matter how hard the test and they were winners in their own right.

When they loss by man's standards he would encourage them to do better the next time around. But the object of the game was to reach the overall prize and to not give up when challenges came. They should not be a bad sport and become disorderly and bring shame on the team. He would say if a member didn't follow the rules of the game they could jeopardize the ultimate winning. Not just for themselves but for many who counted on them. There was so much more to the game and it would take a while for Maylene to learn this new language. For example, what position would she play? The Quarter Back, the Running Back, Receiver, Offensive Line, Defensive Line, Defensive Back or Defensive Safety? G would help her in the area where he seen her greatest skills. And on her own she would study plays of former recorded games to build where she was weak. Being in service on that morning was the beginning of great things. Just as G stayed by Maylene's side she was constantly reminded that she was not alone. That was until the Senior Pastor called Maylene to the front of the church but she was not too sure why. Then he informed the congregation that he learned that one day as she was attending one of the Bro. Gentleman's football practices she helped a few children and their mothers when she shared her profound testimony. She told them about God's favor since she became a single parent. She admitted raising a young child on your own just wasn't easy. As he spoke she recalled the words that she shared.

Maylene: Children do not be discouraged. Things with your mom will work out. We all make mistakes and please know it is not the kids fault.

Football Youth Member: Whoa, you
Ms. Frost, you made mistakes?

Maylene: OHHHH BOY have I. I am far from perfect. But I
aim for perfection and not just living a mediocre life.

Football Youth Member: What about Mr. Frost, don't you
love him anymore? My mom hates my dad. Do all divorce
parents hate their ex?

Maylene: This may be true for some people. But I soon
learned if I didn't forgive and ask for forgiveness I am no
better than the next person who has done wrong. I am not
saying it is easy to do but it is possible.

Football Youth Member: Wow, I will tell my mom this when
I get home!

As a result of this conversation Maylene established a
Women's Group formally known as the SAULS. This was the
code name that the community used to say about the stay at
home house wives. The acronym stood for Stay At Home
Useless Losers. But some caught on and realized they couldn't
be as successful as they had become if it wasn't these ladies
that they spoke down to. They gave them their props and a
new name was established. They became the Sound Authority
1Under Love and their brand became well known around the
community. If it wasn't for what God gave Maylene some of
them could have been stuck in self-pity rather than the new

entrepreneurs that they had become. By this time the Pastor
was in tears. He explained it is not easy to stand naked before
a people who can wrongfully judge you and want you to rot in
your sins. But the mercy of the love of her life showed her
that she is not the only one who has made mistakes and neither
is her former husband. Although they ended their marriage
they both could love again. For this reason, she wants to invite
all of the church to their wedding celebration that would take
place right here at "He Is Love 1" In Attleboro Massachusetts,
better known as Possibilities With A Promise. At this point
Maylene is looking as surprise as the congregation. Then the
pastor went further to say, everyone is asked to wear Black
and White and each of you will serve as their Bridal Party.
By doing this you accept the invitation to participate in their
wedding. It will be at 4 p.m. in the afternoon. Your
attendance will be your confirmed RSVP. Tears began to roll
down the Pastor's face.......

Pastor: Some of you do not know her struggle or her story but
in all of her imperfections someone never forgot her and he
accepted her for who she is. He proposed and had no regrets.
At this point the Pastor could barely keep his composure. He
lifted up his hands and said, no further delay I announce to you
the future bride of the man you know as Gentleman and we
know as JESUS CHRIST! Congratulations my sister. You are
blessed beyond words!!!!! Then out came G all in white. He
was more than her undercover angel. He was amazing! The
Pastor fell to his knees and worshipped God like never before!
The mother's in the church who use to call Gentleman all out
of his name thought that they had seen a ghost. They didn't

realize the very one who they ridiculed were in fact there to bless them. Thankfully G didn't discriminate and he loved them all. Be careful how you judge, we never know who we are entertaining!

To each of you who has gone astray and do not know your way back to the Master's house find a local church that openly talks about God's mercy and is willing to coach you back to life. A church that will embrace you with love and show you that Christ loves all people, no matter your race, religion, sexual preference, or title.
He hates sin and wants us to aim for doing what is good. He is certain to tell you when you are wrong and he will give you a way of escape from any temptation.

We'll see you at the wedding on
First Sunday! God bless you all!

G is Maylene's Psalms 91!

91 He that dwelleth in the secret place of the most High Almighty.
2 I will say of the LORD, He is my refuge and my fortress: my God; in him will I trust.
3 Surely he shall deliver thee from the snare of the fowler, and from the noisome pestilence.

4 He shall cover thee with his feathers, and under his wings shalt thou trust: his truth shall be thy shield and buckler.

5 Thou shalt not be afraid for the terror by night; nor for the arrow that flieth by day;

6 Nor for the pestilence that walketh in darkness; nor for the destruction that wasteth at noonday.

7 A thousand shall fall at thy side, and ten thousand at thy right hand; but it shall not come nigh thee.

8 Only with thine eyes shalt thou behold and see the reward of the wicked.

9 Because thou hast made the LORD, which is my refuge, even the most High, thy habitation;

10 There shall no evil befall thee, neither shall any plague come nigh thy dwelling.

11 For he shall give his angels charge over thee, to keep thee in all thy ways.

12 They shall bear thee up in their hands, lest thou dash thy foot against a stone.

13 Thou shalt tread upon the lion and adder: the young lion and the dragon shalt thou trample under feet.

[14] Because he hath set his love upon me, therefore will I deliver him: I will set him on high, because he hath known my name.

[15] He shall call upon me, and I will answer him: I will be with him in trouble; I will deliver him, and honour him.

[16] With long life will I satisfy him, and shew him my salvation.

Last but not least… a great recipe *I Corinthians 13:4-8*

[4] Love is patient, love is kind. It does not envy, it does not boast, it is not proud. [5] It does not dishonor others, it is not selfseeking, it is not easily angered, it keeps no record of wrongs. [6] Love does not delight in evil but rejoices with the truth. [7] It always protects, always trusts, always hopes, always perseveres. [8] Love never fails.

About The Author

Alecia R. Mullen is an American Ordained Minister,
the daughter of Deacon Walter and Reverend Joyce Harris.
Mrs. Mullen was born and raised in Boston Massachusetts and
reared with her four siblings. She is the proud wife of
James J. Mullen Jr, the mother of six beautiful children and the
grandmother of three precious grandchildren. Mrs. Mullen's
greatest passion is to help those who are in need to the best of
her ability. She believes all things are possible with God when
we BELIEVE!

Made in the USA
Middletown, DE
19 April 2017